cooking
seafood

cooking
seafood

Kathy Knudsen

THUNDER BAY
P·R·E·S·S

San Diego, California

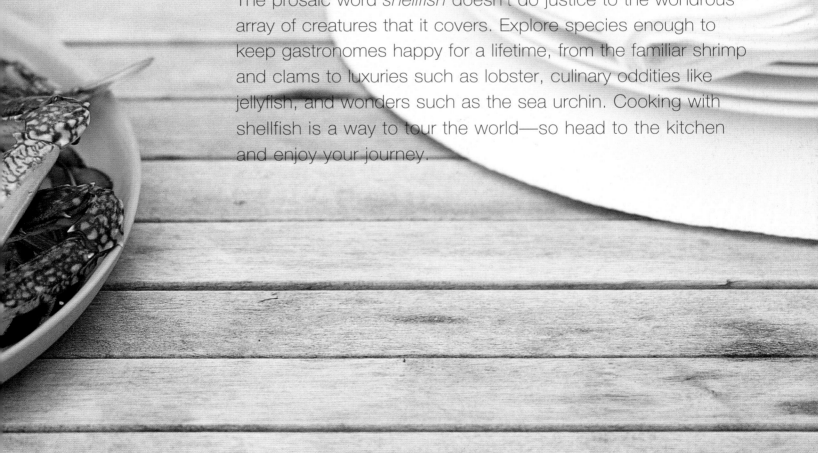

contents

Among the myriad species of fish are mighty salmon, tuna, and kingfish; magnificent reef fish such as snapper and purple-pink pomfret; mottled creatures like ling; flounder, sole, and other curious flat fish; and the slippery eel. Take the plunge at the fishmonger—experiment with these and other delicious species and the many exciting ways in which to cook them.

The prosaic word *shellfish* doesn't do justice to the wondrous array of creatures that it covers. Explore species enough to keep gastronomes happy for a lifetime, from the familiar shrimp and clams to luxuries such as lobster, culinary oddities like jellyfish, and wonders such as the sea urchin. Cooking with shellfish is a way to tour the world—so head to the kitchen and enjoy your journey.

a world of flavor

Visiting a fish market can be an exhilarating experience. With so many beautifully colored creatures of all sizes and shapes, it's wonderful to walk around observing each remarkable species in turn. But the very thing that makes seafood so wondrous—its great variety—also makes it harder to know where to begin. The fish that sparkle so invitingly behind the fish counter can look strange indeed when lying on the kitchen counter at home.

There is little need for hesitation, however, as seafood can be easy to prepare and cook. Preparing seafood offers one of the best ways to explore other cultures and cuisines. And you can leave the fishmongers to gut and scale the fish. The main requirement of fish and shellfish is freshness. For best possible results, buy seafood on the day of eating or, at the latest, the day before. But this is not an insurmountable problem—most large supermarkets have fresh seafood counters and local fishmongers and markets are springing up—give them a try, ask questions, and develop a relationship with the staff. You'll soon know who is the most informed and passionate about their product.

Seafood makes up the world's most numerous and diverse group of "wild" food stocks, and can be found in all the waters of the world—but it is a delicate, finite resource. Unfortunately, worldwide fish stocks in recent decades have been under increasing pressure through overfishing, damage to marine habitats, and wasteful practices like bycatch from commercial fishing. So, what to do? Well, don't stop eating seafood, but be aware of which species are safe to buy and which are endangered. Numerous local and international groups will happily provide information and are making many positive developments: the Marine Stewardship Council, a nonprofit, international organization that awards sustainable fisheries the right to label their products with their logo, offers a clear sign to consumers that these are products worth supporting. Farmed fish and shellfish are another option. Fisheries now demonstrate just what sustainable aquaculture is all about by farming delicious and environmentally friendly kingfish, rainbow trout, mussels, and clams.

The recipes in this book demonstrate how easily seafood can become an exciting and nutritious part of everyday cooking. To maintain this wonderful range of flavors and textures, we as consumers need to play our part in encouraging sustainable fishing practices. That way, tuna skewers can sizzle on our barbecues, and golden-fried cod fillets can accompany our fries and garlicky mayonnaise for a long time to come.

fish

If big supermarkets take the fun out of shopping, the fresh fish counter puts it back in. Few other foods offer such an array of shapes, sizes, colors, and textures. As awareness has grown of the importance of fish in a healthy diet, the quality and range of fish available have improved. Cooking with fish is also a great way to discover different cuisines and new flavor combinations, and to learn new cooking techniques. The recipes that follow reveal something of the versatility and excitement of cooking with fish. Some dishes appear the world over, in different local guises—hearty fish stews, for example, are as popular in the Mediterranean as in Goa. Other dishes are unique to a particular cuisine: teriyaki salmon and barbecued eel with soy mirin glaze are clearly Japanese. Often, it is the accompanying ingredients, not the fish, that reveal the dish's origin—the refreshing mint and lemongrass in a Vietnamese soup, or the harissa, cumin, and turmeric in a spicy Tunisian version.

When buying fish, it can be tempting to choose fillets and cutlets that look healthy and safe, but it is far easier to determine whether a fish is fresh by looking at a whole specimen. Check that the fish smells of the sea—it should not smell "fishy"—that the flesh is firm, the scales are shiny, and the eyes are clear and bright. Really fresh fish may have gaping mouths and open gill flaps, and some fish, such as salmon and trout, are covered in a clear slime (old slime is opaque). When buying fillets, buy from a whole fish if possible, asking your fishmonger to scale, gut, fillet, and skin it for you, if necessary.

A common misconception about cooking with fish is that it is high risk. Fish do cook quickly, so they need to be watched, but this short cooking time should be seen as an advantage. Many fish are excellent when marinated, making them perfect for entertaining; prepare them in advance, or cook them on the barbecue with little or no preparation. The key is to choose the right fish for the cooking technique and to do as much preparation as possible before cooking, so that you don't get distracted at a crucial moment. Firm fish such as salmon and oily fish such as tuna, sardines, and mackerel are great for the barbecue; sole and whiting are classic choices for the pan; and blue-eye cod, John Dory, sea bass, snapper, and bream are all very adaptable and can be fried, steamed, or baked. If you're seeking a challenge, try making sushi hand-rolls or homemade seafood lasagna; your efforts will be well rewarded.

Most recipes in this chapter offer substitute fish if the suggested fish is not available. Always choose good-quality fish, and let the fish do the rest.

smoked tuna and white bean salad
with basil dressing .... serves 4

CANNED TUNA IS POSSIBLY THE ULTIMATE CONVENIENCE SEAFOOD, ALWAYS AT THE READY FOR SANDWICHES, SALADS, OR QUICK PASTA SAUCES. SMOKED FILLETS ARE PARTICULARLY DELICIOUS. THIS MEDITERRANEAN-INSPIRED SALAD IS SIMPLE YET SUBSTANTIAL, PERFECT FOR A SUMMER LUNCH.

arugula	1 small bunch
red bell pepper	1 small, cut into thin batons
red onion	1 small, finely sliced
canned cannellini beans	1³/4 cups, drained and rinsed
cherry tomatoes	1 cup, cut into halves
capers	2 tablespoons, rinsed and squeezed dry
canned smoked tuna slices in oil	1³/4 cups, drained
bread	to serve

basil dressing

lemon juice	1 tablespoon
white wine vinegar	1 tablespoon
extra-virgin olive oil	1/4 cup
garlic	1 clove, crushed
basil	2 tablespoons chopped
sugar	1/2 teaspoon

Trim any long stems from the arugula, rinse, pat dry, and divide among four serving plates.

Lightly toss the bell pepper in a large bowl with the onion, beans, tomatoes, and capers. Spoon some of this mixture onto the arugula on each plate, then sprinkle some tuna over each.

To make the dressing, thoroughly whisk all the ingredients in a bowl with 1 tablespoon water, 1/4 teaspoon salt, and freshly ground black pepper to taste. Drizzle over the salad and serve immediately with bread.

Fish substitution—fresh tuna, seared on both sides and sliced, or canned salmon

Remove the membranes and seeds from the bell pepper

Slice the bell pepper into thin batons

Whisk together all the ingredients for the basil dressing

thai fish cakes .... serves 4-6

THESE CLASSIC THAI APPETIZERS ARE QUICK AND EASY TO MAKE IN A FOOD PROCESSOR. THEY TYPICALLY HAVE A PUFFY APPEARANCE AND ARE FIRM AND SLIGHTLY CHEWY. THEIR FLAVOR IS MILDLY SPICY; IF YOU PREFER A BIT MORE HEAT, INCREASE THE QUANTITY OF RED CURRY PASTE ACCORDING TO YOUR TASTE.

firm white fish fillets, such as ling, cod, or hake	1 pound, skinned
rice flour	1/4 cup
fish sauce	1 tablespoon
egg	1, lightly beaten
cilantro leaves	3 tablespoons
red curry paste	1 tablespoon
red chilies	1–2 teaspoons chopped, optional
green beans	1 1/2 cups, very thinly sliced
scallions	2, finely chopped
oil	for frying
sweet chili sauce	to serve
chopped peanuts and finely diced cucumber	to garnish, optional

Roughly chop the fish into chunks, then process in a food processor for 20 seconds or until smooth.

Add the rice flour, fish sauce, egg, cilantro leaves, curry paste, and chilies, if using. Blend for 10 seconds or until well combined, then transfer to a large bowl. Alternatively, finely chop and blend by hand. Mix in the green beans and scallions. With wet hands, form 2 tablespoons of mixture at a time into flattish patties about 2 inches in diameter.

Heat the oil in a heavy-based frying pan over medium heat. Cook four fish cakes at a time until golden brown on both sides. Drain on crumpled paper towels, then serve with sweet chili sauce. The sauce can be garnished with a sprinkle of chopped peanuts and finely diced cucumber, if you wish.

Roughly chop the fish fillets into large chunks

Put the fish into a food processor and blend until smooth

Using wet hands, form the mixture into flattish patties

sardines with caesar salad .... serves 4

HERE, THE ANCHOVIES USUALLY INCLUDED IN CAESAR SALAD ARE COMBINED WITH CRUMBED, FRIED SARDINES. SCALED AND BUTTERFLIED SARDINES ARE AVAILABLE IN VACUUM PACKS AT SOME FISHMONGERS. INSTRUCTIONS ARE GIVEN BELOW FOR PREPARING YOUR OWN, OR ASK YOUR FISHMONGER TO DO IT FOR YOU.

dressing

egg	1
garlic	2 cloves
lemon juice	2 tablespoons
Worcestershire sauce	1/2 teaspoon
anchovy fillets	3–4
extra-virgin olive oil	1/2 cup
dry bread crumbs	1 cup
Parmesan cheese	2/3 cup grated
Italian parsley	2 tablespoons chopped
eggs	2, lightly beaten
milk	1/3 cup
sardines	16, scaled and butterflied
oil	for deep-frying
poppadoms	12 small
romaine lettuce	2 heads, leaves separated
prosciutto	8 slices, cooked until crisp, then broken into pieces
Parmesan cheese	1/2 cup shaved

To make the dressing, put the egg in a food processor, add the garlic, lemon juice, Worcestershire sauce, and anchovies, and process to combine. With the motor running, add the oil in a thin, steady stream until the dressing has thickened slightly. Set aside.

Put the bread crumbs, grated Parmesan, and parsley in a bowl and mix well. Put the beaten eggs and milk in another bowl and whisk well. Dip the sardines into the egg wash, then into the crumb mixture, and put on a paper-lined baking sheet. Refrigerate for 1 hour.

Heat the oil in a deep fryer or heavy-based frying pan to 350°F or until a cube of white bread dropped into the oil browns in 15 seconds. Deep-fry the poppadoms until crisp, drain on paper towels, then break into pieces. Deep-fry the sardines in batches until crisp and golden.

Arrange the lettuce, prosciutto, poppadoms, and shaved Parmesan on serving plates, drizzle with dressing, and top with the sardines.

Fish substitution—small herring, mackerel

Sleek, silver sardines belong to the herring family, which also includes anchovies. Sardines are found all over the world, but are particularly popular in the Mediterranean. They are fairly fatty, so are ideal for barbecuing. They can also be marinated, baked, stuffed, smoked, or canned. Sardines can be butterflied by boning through the back or the belly, with the head left on or removed. To butterfly sardines through the back, lay the scaled fish on its side and cut from the head to the tail along its back with a sharp knife, keeping the knife flat against the bones. Repeat on the other side, taking care not to cut through the belly. Snip the bones at the tail and head, pull the bones free, and remove the guts. Pat clean.

marinated herring with mustard and tarragon

MARINATED HERRING ARE A POPULAR SNACK IN THE NETHERLANDS, BELGIUM, AND SCANDINAVIA. THEY ARE OFTEN EATEN RAW, BUT IN THIS RECIPE, AN ACIDIC MARINADE SERVES TO "COLD-COOK" THEM. THEY MAKE A DELICIOUS LIGHT LUNCH WITH WHEAT BREAD AND BUTTER.

herrings	4, filleted
pickling spice	1 tablespoon
bay leaves	2
black peppercorns	6
onion	1, cut in half lengthwise and thinly sliced
white wine vinegar	3/4 cup
soft brown sugar	1 teaspoon
whole-grain mustard	1 tablespoon
tarragon	2 tablespoons chopped
wheat bread and butter	to serve

Preheat the oven to 300°F. Season the herring fillets with salt and pepper. Roll up each fillet, secure with a toothpick, and place in a single layer in a baking dish that is just large enough to hold the rolled herrings.

Put the pickling spice, bay leaves, peppercorns, onion, vinegar, and sugar into a saucepan with 1 1/2 cups water and bring to a boil. Remove the pan from the heat and stir in the mustard and tarragon.

Pour the liquid over the rolled herring fillets. Cover with foil and bake in the preheated oven for 45 minutes. Allow to completely cool in the liquid before removing them from the marinade and serving cold with wheat bread and butter.

Fish substitution—mackerel fillets

Roll up the fillets and secure each with a toothpick

Stir the mustard and tarragon into the pickling liquid

three ways with salmon

VERSATILE AND DELICIOUS, SALMON CAN BE SERVED RAW, COOKED, OR SMOKED. SMOKED SALMON IS NOW READILY AVAILABLE IN SUPERMARKETS. IT'S NOT CHEAP, BUT A LITTLE GOES A LONG WAY AND TRANSFORMS A SIMPLE SALAD, SUCH AS THE FOLLOWING ARUGULA DISH, INTO SOMETHING SPECIAL. IF SERVING SALMON RAW, ASK FOR CARPACCIO. BUY THE FRESHEST, BEST-QUALITY SALMON YOU CAN FIND. SALMON WITH A RICH, STICKY TERIYAKI MARINADE MAKES FOR A QUICK, ELEGANT DINNER WITH A JAPANESE TOUCH.

smoked salmon and arugula salad

To make the dressing, thoroughly whisk together 2 tablespoons extra-virgin olive oil and 1 tablespoon balsamic vinegar in a bowl. Season to taste. Trim the long stems from 1 bunch arugula. Rinse the leaves, pat dry, and gently toss in a bowl with the dressing. Cut 1 avocado into 12 wedges. Put 3 wedges on each plate. Divide 9 ounces smoked salmon slices and the arugula among the plates. Sprinkle 2 cups drained and crumbled marinated goat cheese and 2 tablespoons roughly chopped roasted hazelnuts over the top. Season with freshly ground black pepper. Serves 4.

Fish substitution—smoked trout

salmon carpaccio

Wrap a 1-pound, 2-ounce sashimi-grade piece of salmon in foil and freeze for 20–30 minutes or until partly frozen. Meanwhile, score a cross in the base of 3 vine-ripened tomatoes. Cover with boiling water for 30 seconds, then plunge into cold water. Drain and peel. Cut each tomato in half, scoop out the seeds with a teaspoon, and dice the flesh. Put the flesh in a bowl and stir in 1 tablespoon chopped dill and 1 tablespoon baby capers, rinsed and squeezed dry. Remove the salmon from the freezer and unwrap. Using a very sharp knife, carefully slice the salmon thinly across the grain. Cover four serving plates with a thin layer of the slices. Whisk together 1 tablespoon extra-virgin olive oil, 1 tablespoon lime juice, and a large pinch of sea salt. Drizzle over the salmon just before serving. Season with freshly ground pepper and serve immediately with the tomato mixture and crusty bread. Serves 4.

Fish substitution—fresh tuna, smoked salmon

teriyaki salmon

In a pitcher, mix together 1/3 cup soy sauce, 1/3 cup sake, 1/3 cup mirin, 1 teaspoon sesame oil, 2 tablespoons soft brown sugar, 2 teaspoons finely grated fresh ginger, and 1 crushed small garlic clove. Place four 7-ounce salmon fillets in a shallow nonmetallic dish and pour the marinade over them. Turn the fillets in the marinade so that they are well coated. Cover and leave to marinate in the refrigerator for at least 3 hours. Heat 1 tablespoon oil in a large, heavy-based frying pan. Remove the salmon from the marinade and drain on paper towels. Fry the salmon in the oil until browned on each side, then reduce the heat and cook for 3 minutes more or until the salmon is just cooked through. Add the marinade and bring to a simmer. Remove the fish and simmer the sauce until it is thick and sticky. Return the salmon to the pan, quickly coat with the sauce, and then transfer to serving plates. Garnish with 2 trimmed and chopped scallions and serve with rice. Serves 4.

Fish substitution—ocean trout

smoked salmon and arugula salad

barbecued eel with
soy mirin glaze

. . . . serves 4

FRESHWATER EEL COOKED UNDER THE BROILER OR ON THE BARBECUE AND COATED WITH A SWEET SOY SAUCE GLAZE IS TENDER AND DELICIOUS. IF THE FILLETS ARE LONG AND YOU ARE USING THE BARBECUE, PUT A SKEWER SIDEWAYS THROUGH BOTH ENDS OF EACH FILLET; THIS WILL MAKE THEM EASIER TO TURN.

Japanese soy sauce	1/3 cup
mirin	1/3 cup
superfine sugar	2 tablespoons
cucumber	1/4
daikon radish	1/4
freshwater eel fillets	4 x 6-ounce, skinned
cooked white rice	to serve

Put the soy sauce, mirin, and superfine sugar into a small saucepan. Bring the liquid slowly to a boil and heat for 5–6 minutes, until the liquid has reduced by approximately half and is thick and syrupy. Remove the pan from the heat. Preheat the broiler or barbecue to high.

Meanwhile, peel and finely shred the cucumber and daikon. Mix together.

Cook the eel for 2 minutes on each side, then brush liberally with the sauce. Continue to cook for 2–3 minutes on each side. Turn the eel frequently, brushing with the sauce to create a glaze. Serve the eel with the cucumber and daikon garnish.

Fish substitution—mackerel

With a large, sharp knife, remove roots and stem from the daikon

Peel and finely shred the cucumber and daikon

Brush the eel liberally with the glaze while cooking

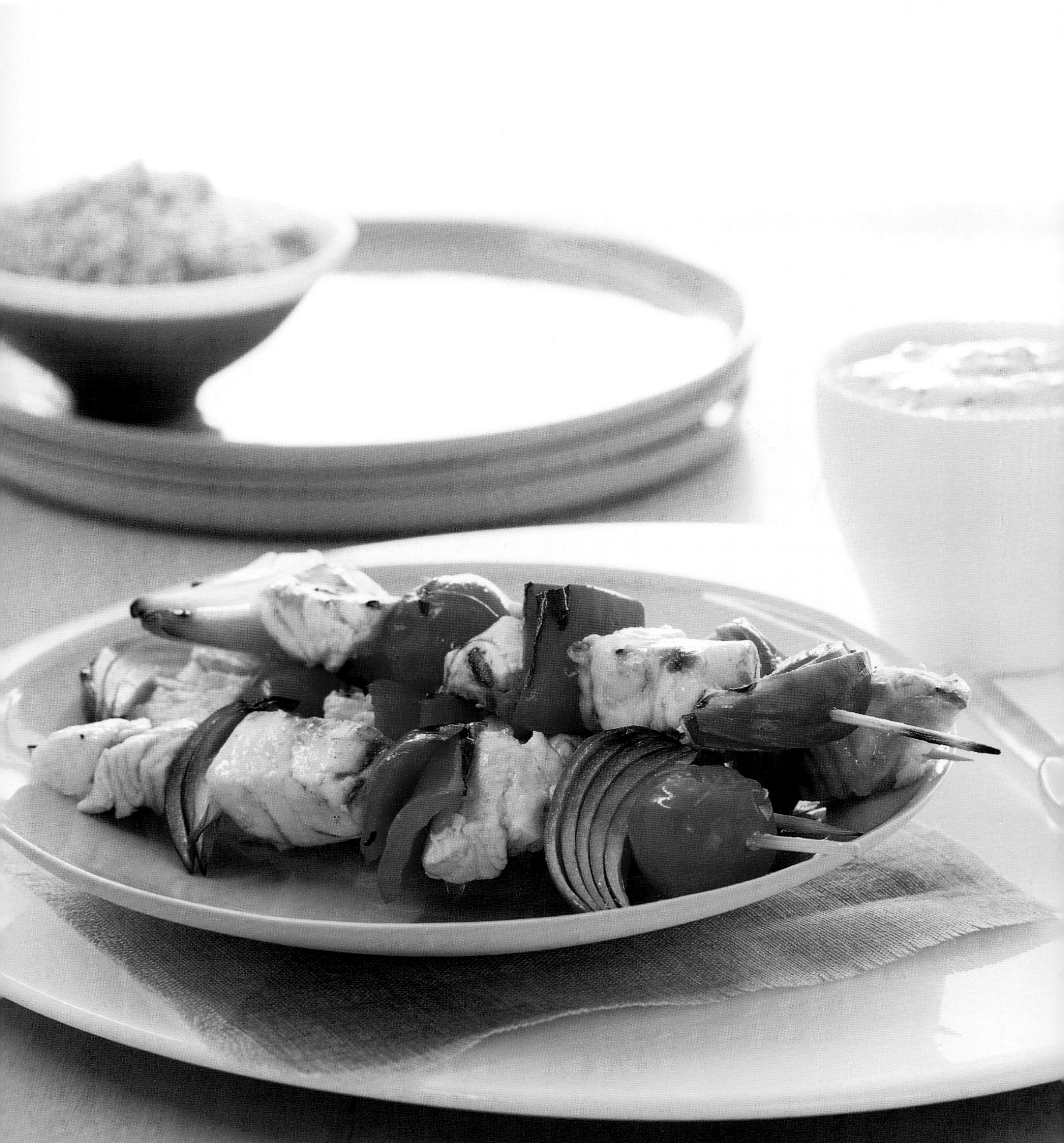

barramundi kabobs with lemon and herb yogurt

NATIVE TO THE COASTAL REGIONS OF NORTHERN AUSTRALIA, BARRAMUNDI IS MILDLY FLAVORED, WITH MOIST, FIRM FLESH THAT HAS A LARGE FLAKE. A VERSATILE FISH, IT LENDS ITSELF WELL TO A VARIETY OF COOKING METHODS. IF YOU CAN'T FIND BARRAMUNDI, SWORDFISH IS A GOOD SUBSTITUTE.

barramundi fillet	1-pound, 12-ounce, skinless, cut into 1¼-inch chunks
lemon juice	⅓ cup
olive oil	⅓ cup
bay leaves	3
cherry tomatoes	16
red onions	2 small, each cut into 8 wedges
red or orange bell peppers	2 small, seeded and each cut into 8 chunks

lemon and herb yogurt

yogurt	a heaping ¾ cup
lemon juice	1 tablespoon
paprika	a pinch
mint	1 tablespoon finely chopped
Italian parsley	1 tablespoon finely chopped

COUSCOUS

instant couscous	2¼ cups
fish or vegetable stock	1⅔ cups, brought to a boil
olive oil	1 tablespoon
butter	1½ tablespoons

Place the fish chunks in a nonmetallic bowl with the lemon juice, olive oil, and bay leaves. Toss to mix, cover, and leave to marinate for about 30 minutes in the refrigerator.

To make the lemon and herb yogurt, put all the ingredients in a small bowl and whisk together. Refrigerate until needed.

On each of eight metal skewers, or bamboo skewers that have been soaked for 30 minutes, thread three or four chunks of fish, two cherry tomatoes, two pieces of onion, and two pieces of bell pepper, alternating between the fish and the various vegetables as you go.

Preheat the barbecue or charbroil pan to high. Brush the kabobs lightly with oil, then cook for 8–10 minutes. Baste with the remaining marinade as they cook, and turn occasionally. When ready, the fish should be firm and opaque and the vegetables slightly charred.

Meanwhile, put the couscous into a heatproof bowl, add the stock and oil, cover tightly, and leave to sit for 5 minutes or according to the manufacturer's directions. Fluff the grains with a fork and stir in the butter. Serve the kabobs on a mound of couscous, accompanied by the yogurt dressing.

Fish substitution—tuna, flake, kingfish, swordfish

Seed the bell pepper and chop it into chunks

Toss together the fish, lemon juice, olive oil, and bay leaves

Thread alternating chunks of fish and vegetables onto skewers

sugar-cured salmon . . . . serves 4

SALMON FILLETS ARE CURED USING A SUGAR, SALT, AND HERB MIXTURE OVER A PERIOD OF TWO DAYS. THIS RECIPE IS SIMILAR TO THE TRADITIONAL SCANDINAVIAN DISH OF GRAVLAX. LIKE GRAVLAX, IT IS EATEN RAW AND SERVED WITH A MUSTARD SAUCE.

middle salmon fillet	1-pound piece, skinless
soft brown sugar	1 cup
coarse sea salt	1 cup
black peppercorns	8, lightly crushed
dill	1 tablespoon chopped
tarragon	1 tablespoon chopped
basil	1 tablespoon shredded

mustard sauce

egg yolks	3, at room temperature
light olive oil	2/3 cup
peanut oil	2/3 cup
zest	of 1 lemon, finely grated
lemon juice	1 tablespoon
dill	3 tablespoons chopped
whole-grain mustard	2 teaspoons
heavy cream	1/3 cup

Place the salmon on a board and check for bones. Bones left in the salmon will make slicing the fish thinly difficult, as the bones will catch on the knife. Any small, stubborn bones can be removed using tweezers.

Mix the sugar and salt together and spoon half of the mixture into a shallow rectangular nonmetallic dish large enough to hold the salmon. Place the fish on the mixture. Sprinkle the peppercorns, dill, tarragon, and basil over the fish. Cover with the remaining sugar and salt mixture. Cover loosely with plastic wrap. Then place a tray, small board, or plate on top of the fish, with a couple of cans to weigh it down. Refrigerate for 2 days, turning the fish over in the mixture every 12 hours.

To make the sauce, place the egg yolks in a medium-sized bowl with a generous pinch of salt and freshly ground black pepper, and gently whisk together. Mix the oils together in a pitcher. Slowly add the oil to the egg yolks, drop by drop, whisking all the time. Increase to a slow trickle as the sauce thickens.

Fold in the lemon zest and juice, dill, and mustard. Whisk the cream until slightly fluffy, then fold into the mixture. Taste and season with extra salt and pepper if desired.

Remove the fish from the dish and brush off the sugar and salt. Discard any brine. Using a sharp knife and cutting along the length of the piece of salmon, slice into paper-thin pieces and serve with the mustard sauce. The sugar-cured salmon will keep in the refrigerator for 2 days.

Fish substitution—ocean trout

three ways with fish soup

HARISSA, A FIERY MIXTURE OF UP TO TWENTY SPICES, IS USED IN MIDDLE EASTERN AND NORTH AFRICAN COOKING. HERE IT FLAVORS A SPICY SOUP FROM TUNISIA. SOUR-TASTING SAUCES AND SOUPS SUCH AS THE FOLLOWING RECIPE ARE COMMON TO VIETNAMESE COOKING, AS IS THE ADDITION OF HERBS, PARTICULARLY MINT AND LEMONGRASS. THE VERMICELLI FISH SOUP IS A POPULAR DISH FROM LAOS; IT IS SERVED IN THE MIDDLE OR AT THE END OF A MEAL, OR EVEN AT BREAKFAST. THIS RECIPE WORKS WELL WITH ANY FIRM WHITE FISH.

tunisian fish soup

Heat $1/4$ cup olive oil in a large saucepan. Add 1 chopped onion and 1 chopped celery stalk and cook for 8–10 minutes or until softened. Add 4 crushed garlic cloves and cook for an additional minute. Stir in 2 tablespoons concentrated tomato purée, $1 1/2$ teaspoons ground turmeric, $1 1/2$ teaspoons ground cumin, and 2 teaspoons harissa, and cook for 30 seconds, stirring constantly. Pour 4 cups fish stock into the saucepan and add 2 bay leaves. Bring to a boil, then reduce the heat to low and simmer gently for 15 minutes. Add 1 cup orzo or other small pasta to the liquid and cook for about 10 minutes or until al dente. Cut 1 pound, 2 ounces mixed skinless snapper and sea bass fillets into bite-sized chunks and add to the liquid. Poach gently for 3–4 minutes or until the fish is opaque. Stir in 2 tablespoons chopped mint and 2 tablespoons lemon juice, season to taste with salt, then serve with warm pita bread. Garnish with a few extra mint leaves, if desired. Serves 6.

vietnamese sour fish soup

Cut 1 pound filleted and skinless fish such as snapper, cod, or triggerfish into bite-sized pieces. Cover and refrigerate until required. Meanwhile, score a cross in the base of 2 vine-ripened tomatoes. Cover with boiling water for 30 seconds, then plunge into cold water. Drain and peel the skin away from the cross. Cut each tomato into 8 pieces. Heat $1/4$ cup oil in a large saucepan and when hot, add 1 finely chopped large garlic clove, 2 finely sliced shallots, 1 very finely chopped stem lemongrass (white part only), and 2 carrots, peeled and cut into thin, $2 1/2$-inch-long batons. Cook on a medium heat for 10 minutes or until softened, stirring occasionally. Add 3 cups fish stock or water, 2 tablespoons tamarind purée, 1 teaspoon sambal oelek or other chili sauce, $1/4$ cup fish sauce, and $1/4$ teaspoon sugar. Bring to a boil and then reduce the heat to low and simmer for 5 minutes. Add the fish and tomato pieces, $1 1/2$ cups bean sprouts, and 2 trimmed and finely shredded scallions. Cook for an additional 5 minutes or until the fish is opaque. Stir in the juice of 1 lime, 2 tablespoons roughly chopped roasted peanuts, and 3 tablespoons chopped Vietnamese mint. Serves 4.

vermicelli fish soup

Cut 14 ounces firm white fish fillets such as cod, sea bass, haddock, halibut, perch, or bream into thick strips. Cover and refrigerate until needed. Put $1 1/4$ cups bean thread or rice vermicelli in a bowl and cover with boiling water. Leave to soak for 10 minutes or until completely tender, then drain and cut into short lengths. Meanwhile, put $1 2/3$ cups fish stock in a large saucepan and bring to a boil. Reduce the heat to low and add $1 1/4$ cups coconut milk and simmer for 5 minutes. Add $1 1/2$ cups thinly sliced mushrooms and 1 thinly sliced small red chili. Cook for 30 seconds, then add the fish and $3/4$ cup shredded young spinach leaves. Poach for 2 minutes. Carefully stir in the noodles, along with 1 tablespoon soy sauce, 2 tablespoons fish sauce, the zest and juice of 1 lime, $3/4$ cup bean sprouts, $2/3$ cup thinly sliced cucumber, 2 trimmed and chopped scallions, and 2 tablespoons chopped mint. Heat through and serve. Serves 6.

sushi hand-rolls . . . . serves 4

NORI (OR LAVER) IS AN EDIBLE SEAWEED THAT IS GREATLY APPRECIATED BY THE JAPANESE. NORI IS SOLD DRIED IN PAPER-THIN SHEETS OR IN FLAKES. IT IS USED FOR WRAPPING SUSHI, SHREDDED INTO SOUPS, OR CRUMBLED ONTO RICE. THE SHEETS SHOULD BE GENTLY TOASTED BEFORE USE TO RELEASE THE DELICATE SWEET FLAVOR.

sushi rice	1 cup
rice vinegar	2 tablespoons
superfine sugar	a generous pinch
very fresh fish, such as salmon fillet or tuna	6 ounces, skinless
toasted nori (dried seaweed)	6 sheets, each 8 x 7 inches
avocado	1 small
lemon juice	1 tablespoon
wasabi paste	to taste
pickled daikon radish	1/2 cup
cucumber	2/3 cup, cut into thin strips
Japanese soy sauce	to serve
pickled ginger	to serve

Rinse the rice under cold running water until it runs clear. Put the rice into a saucepan with 1 cup cold water. Cover the pan, bring to a boil, reduce the heat, and simmer for 10 minutes.

Meanwhile, combine 1 tablespoon of the vinegar, the sugar, and 1/4 teaspoon of salt. When the rice is cooked, remove from the heat and let it stand covered for 10 minutes. Transfer to a mixing bowl. Gradually add the rice vinegar mixture, turning and folding the rice using a wooden spoon or spatula, until the rice is cool. Cover with a damp dishcloth and set aside; do not refrigerate.

Cut the fish into 12 pieces, about 3/4 x 2 x 1/8 inches. Cut each sheet of nori in half. Thinly slice the avocado and sprinkle with lemon juice. Mix the remaining tablespoon of rice vinegar with 3 tablespoons of water in a small bowl. Use this mixture to keep the rice from sticking to your fingers as you form the sushi. Mold 1 tablespoon of rice at a time into oval shapes—you should end up with 12.

Holding a piece of nori in the palm of your hand, smear a little wasabi over it, place an oval of rice on top, and then top with a piece each of fish, avocado, daikon, and cucumber. Wrap the seaweed around the filling in a cone shape, using a couple of grains of cooked rice as glue to secure the rolls. Alternatively, place the ingredients on the table for guests to help themselves. Serve the sushi with soy sauce, extra wasabi, and pickled ginger.

Mold 1 tablespoon of rice at a time into an oval shape

Top the rice with the fish, avocado, daikon, and cucumber

Roll the nori around the filling to form a neat cone

barbecued salmon cutlets
with sweet cucumber dressing..........................serves 4

THIS RECIPE IS THE WORK OF MINUTES—PERFECT FOR A QUICK YET IMPRESSIVE MEAL. BE CAREFUL NOT TO OVERCOOK THE FISH OR IT WILL BE DRY; IT SHOULD STILL BE A LITTLE PINK IN THE CENTER. ASK YOUR FISHMONGER FOR A CUT FROM THE CENTER OF THE FILLET, AS THIS IS THE BEST PART.

short cucumbers	2 small, peeled, seeded, and finely diced
red onion	1, finely chopped
red chili	1, finely chopped
pickled ginger	2 tablespoons shredded
rice vinegar	2 tablespoons
sesame oil	1/2 teaspoon
salmon cutlets	4
nori (dried seaweed)	1 sheet, toasted and thinly sliced
steamed rice	to serve

Combine the cucumber, onion, chili, ginger, rice vinegar, and sesame oil in a bowl. Cover and set aside at room temperature while cooking the salmon cutlets.

Preheat the barbecue or charbroil pan to high. Lightly brush the salmon cutlets with oil. Cook the salmon on the barbecue or pan for about 2 minutes on each side or until cooked as desired. Serve the salmon topped with the cucumber dressing and sprinkled with the strips of toasted nori. Serve with steamed rice.

Fish substitution—ocean trout cutlets

Peel, seed, and finely dice the cucumbers

Using scissors, cut the toasted nori sheet into thin strips

Cook the fish until just done and still slightly pink in the center

salmon on skordalia
with saffron and lime butter . . . . serves 4

THERE ARE MANY VERSIONS OF SKORDALIA, A GREEK DISH BASED ON BREAD OR POTATOES, OLIVE OIL, AND GARLIC. HERE IT FORMS A BED FOR SALMON WITH A ZESTY BUTTER SAUCE. MASH THE POTATOES WITH A POTATO MASHER; A FOOD PROCESSOR WILL PRODUCE A GLUEY CONSISTENCY.

skordalia

potatoes	1 pound, 2 ounces, peeled and diced
garlic	3 cloves, finely chopped
lime juice	2 tablespoons
milk	1/2 cup
extra-virgin olive oil	2/3 cup

saffron and lime butter

butter	1/4 cup
saffron threads	a pinch
lime juice	2 tablespoons
salmon fillets	4 x 7 ounces
oil	2 tablespoons
lime zest	1 tablespoon grated, to garnish
chervil leaves	to garnish

To make the skordalia, bring a large saucepan of water to a boil, add the potato, and cook for 10 minutes or until very soft. Drain thoroughly and mash until quite smooth. Stir the garlic, lime juice, and milk into the potato, then gradually pour in the oil, mixing well with a wooden spoon.

To make the saffron and lime butter, melt the butter in a small saucepan, add the saffron and lime juice, and cook until the butter turns a nutty brown color. Remove from the heat.

Pat the salmon fillets dry. Heat the oil in a frying pan and cook the salmon, skin side down, over high heat for 2–3 minutes or until the skin is crisp and golden. Turn over and cook for another 2–3 minutes. Serve the salmon on a bed of the skordalia, with the saffron and lime butter drizzled over the top. Garnish with lime zest and chervil leaves.

Fish substitution—ocean trout

The most expensive spice in the world, saffron is the orange-red stigma handpicked from the flower of one species of crocus, and dried. It has a pungent and aromatic flavor and an intense color. It is added to butters and sauces such as hollandaise and aioli, and is a lovely complement to shellfish. Bouillabaisse, paella, the pilafs of India, and Persian dishes all feature saffron. The best comes from Spain, Iran, and Kashmir. Both thread and powder forms are available, but threads are preferable, as the powder can be adulterated with cheaper spices. To use, soak threads in warm water for a few minutes to infuse, then strain the liquid or add both the liquid and the threads to the dish.

pâté shchutei .... serves 4

THIS TERRINE HAS A SOFT TEXTURE AND IS DELICATELY FLAVORED WITH DILL AND CHIVES. IT MAKES AN ELEGANT FIRST COURSE. SERVE EACH SLICE SPRINKLED WITH A LITTLE CAVIAR AND ACCOMPANIED BY A CLEAN-TASTING SALAD, SUCH AS WATERCRESS AND CUCUMBER, RATHER THAN BREAD OR TOASTS.

pike fillet	14 ounces, skinless
egg whites	2 large
heavy cream	1 cup
lemon juice	1 tablespoon
dill	1 tablespoon chopped
chives	1 teaspoon chopped
ground nutmeg	a pinch
salmon fillet	3³/4 ounces, skinless
salmon roe	to garnish, optional

Cut the pike into bite-sized pieces and chill well.

Prepare a loaf pan 8¹/2 x 2³/4 x 2³/4 inches by lining it with baking paper and lightly oiling the paper. Using a food processor, blend the pike to a smooth paste. Add the egg whites, cream, lemon juice, dill, and chives. Process briefly using the pulse. Season with salt, white pepper, and nutmeg. Alternatively, chop the fish very finely by hand and mix with the other ingredients.

Preheat the oven to 350°F. Transfer half of the pike mixture to the loaf pan. Cut the salmon into short, thin strips. Place the salmon strips on top, all facing the same direction so the pâté will cut easily. Season with salt and white pepper and cover with the remaining pike mixture. Cover with foil and place in a roasting pan. Add boiling water until one third of the loaf pan is immersed in water. You may find it easier to add the boiling water to the pan once the pan is in the oven.

Bake in the preheated oven for 40–45 minutes or until firm to the touch. Remove the pan from the water and leave until cold. Chill overnight in the fridge. Place a large plate over the top of the pan and invert both so that the terrine comes out onto the plate. Peel off the paper and serve in slices.

Fish substitution—trout or carp

Process the pike to a fine paste in a food processor

Transfer half of the pike mixture to the lined loaf pan

Spread the remaining pike mixture over the salmon slices

three ways with sauces

THE KAFFIR LIME LEAF AND RED CURRY SAUCE CREATES A HOT SAUCE THAT CAN ALSO BE USED FOR SHELLFISH, PARTICULARLY SHRIMP. IT IS POPULAR IN THAILAND, WHERE IT IS KNOWN AS *CHUCHI*. THE TROPICAL HERB AND YOGURT DRESSING KEEPS FISH LOVELY AND MOIST DURING COOKING. IT IS A SINDHI RECIPE AND USES HILSA (A TYPE OF SHAD), BUT YOU CAN EASILY SUBSTITUTE ANY TYPE OF FLAT FISH. THE BUTTER SAUCE GOES WELL WITH ANY WHITE-FLESHED FISH WITH A FINE TO MEDIUM TEXTURE, SUCH AS FLATHEAD.

kaffir lime leaf and red curry sauce

Heat a wok or pan and add $1/3$ cup oil. Heat the oil until it begins to smoke, then add 2 large crushed garlic cloves and cook for 30 seconds, stirring all the time. Add 1–2 tablespoons red curry paste to taste, and fry for 30 seconds. Add $1 1/4$ cups coconut milk and mix through. Add $1/3$ cup fish sauce, 2 tablespoons sugar, and 2 teaspoons lemon juice, and heat through. Stir in 2 finely shredded kaffir lime leaves and 2 tablespoons chopped cilantro leaves. Spoon over cooked shrimp or skinless fish fillets such as pomfret, sole, or flounder. To prepare the fish, put $1/3$ cup oil in a large wok or frying pan until hot. Add 1 pound, 5 ounces skinless fillets, in batches if necessary, and cook for 2–3 minutes or until opaque. If cooking in batches, transfer the cooked fish to a plate and cover with foil while you cook the remainder. Serves 4.

tropical herb and yogurt dressing

Grate a $1 1/2$-inch piece of fresh ginger. Mix together the ginger, $2 3/4$ cups finely chopped onions, $1 1/4$ cups chopped cilantro leaves, 4–6 finely chopped green chilies, 1 tablespoon ground coriander, $1/2$ teaspoon ground turmeric, and 1 cup plain yogurt. Stir in 1 tablespoon oil. (If you would like a smoother paste, put everything through the blender for a few seconds.) This dressing goes well with such fish as sole, hilsa, bony bream, and pomfret. To use the dressing, put 3 pounds, 5 ounces fish fillets, skin side down, in a shallow ovenproof dish. (If using hilsa or bream fillets, use tweezers to remove any small bones you can feel; they are notoriously bony fish.) Drizzle a little lime juice over the fillets, sprinkle with a pinch of salt, and rub the salt in well. Cover and refrigerate for 1 hour. Preheat the oven to 350°F. Pour the yogurt mixture over the fillets, making sure they are completely coated. Bake for 20 minutes or until the fish flakes when tested with a knife. Serves 6.

french butter sauce

Put $1 2/3$ cups fish stock, $1/3$ cup dry white wine, 1 tablespoon white wine vinegar, 1 finely chopped French shallot, 1 bay leaf, and 1 Italian parsley sprig in a small saucepan. Bring to a boil over high heat, then reduce the heat to medium and simmer until the liquid has reduced by two-thirds. Meanwhile, preheat the broiler to high and cover the broiler tray with foil. Lightly brush the foil with 2 teaspoons oil. Cut $2/3$ cup cold unsalted butter into small cubes. Place on a plate and refrigerate. Sieve the sauce, discarding the shallot and herbs. Return the sauce to the saucepan. Add $3/4$ cup heavy cream and heat until reduced by half. Put 1 pound, 12 ounces skinless fillets such as flathead, snapper, John Dory, or haddock on the broiler tray. Drizzle with the juice of half a lemon and season with salt and freshly ground black pepper. Broil for 7–10 minutes or until the fish is opaque and just cooked through. Meanwhile, finish the sauce: keeping the sauce simmering but not boiling, add the butter, cube by cube, to the sauce, whisking thoroughly after each addition. Stir in 2 tablespoons finely chopped Italian parsley and season with salt and black pepper. Serve the fish with some sauce drizzled over the top; put any remaining sauce in a serving pitcher. Serves 4.

kedgeree

THIS TRADITIONAL ENGLISH BREAKFAST DISH IS BASED ON AN INDIAN RECIPE. WHEN BUYING SMOKED FISH, SELECT THICK PIECES FROM THE CENTER OF THE FILLET. BRIGHT YELLOW OR ORANGE SMOKED FISH HAS BEEN DYED; LOOK FOR THE PALER, UNDYED VARIETY, WHICH HAS BEEN SMOKED FOR LONGER AND HAS A BETTER FLAVOR.

smoked haddock or cod	12 ounces
lemon	3 slices
bay leaf	1
milk	1 1/4 cups
long-grain rice	a heaping 3/4 cup
butter	1/4 cup
onion	1 small, finely chopped
mild curry powder	2 teaspoons
Italian parsley	1 tablespoon finely chopped
eggs	3 hard-boiled, roughly chopped
heavy cream	2/3 cup
mango chutney	to serve

Put the smoked fish in a deep-frying pan with the lemon slices and bay leaf. Cover with the milk and simmer for 6 minutes or until cooked through. Remove the fish with a slotted spoon and break into large flakes. Discard any bones.

Put the rice in a saucepan along with 1 1/2 cups water. Bring to a boil, cover, and cook for 10 minutes or until just cooked—there should be steam holes in the rice. Drain any excess water and fluff up the rice with a fork.

Melt the butter in a frying pan over medium heat. Add the onion and cook for 3 minutes or until soft. Add the curry powder and cook for an additional 2 minutes. Add the rice and carefully stir through, cooking for 2–3 minutes or until heated through. Add the fish, parsley, eggs, and cream, and stir until heated through. Season well with freshly ground black pepper. Serve immediately with mango chutney.

Fish substitution—smoked cod fillets

Chutney is usually understood in the West to mean a sweet, spicy, cooked preserve of vinegar, sugar, spices, and fruit. However, this type (generally store-bought) is a world away from the original Indian version, which may be more of a paste, and is traditionally hand-ground on a stone. Fresh ingredients are used, such as ginger, chilies, onion, garlic, cilantro, coconut, seed spices, or anything else considered piquant or refreshing. Commercially produced mango chutney uses underripe mangoes with such spices as chili, ginger, and cumin to make a mildly spicy relish that is the typical accompaniment for kedgeree, as well as for various curries.

salmon coulibiac .... serves 6

TRADITIONALLY THIS RUSSIAN PIE WOULD USE A YEAST DOUGH RATHER THAN A FLAKY PASTRY DOUGH. THE FILLING ALMOST ALWAYS CONTAINS FISH ALONG WITH HARD-BOILED EGGS, DILL, AND PARSLEY; THIS VERSION ADDS MUSHROOMS. TRY TO BUY SALMON FILLETS CUT FROM THE CENTER RATHER THAN THE TAIL END OF THE FISH.

basmati rice	1/3 cup
eggs	2 hard-boiled, chopped
dill	2 tablespoons chopped
Italian parsley	2 tablespoons chopped
heavy cream	1/4 cup
butter	1/4 cup
onion	1, finely chopped
button mushrooms	3 cups, sliced
lemon juice	2 tablespoons
salmon fillet	1 pound, 2 ounces center-cut piece, skinless
frozen puff pastry	1 pound, 2 ounces, thawed
egg	1, lightly beaten

Cook the rice in boiling salted water until just al dente, then drain and transfer to a bowl. When cooled slightly, add the chopped hard-boiled egg, dill, and parsley, season with salt and freshly ground black pepper, and stir in the cream.

Melt half the butter in a frying pan and add the onion. Cook for 5 minutes or until soft but not brown. Add the mushrooms and cook for 5 minutes or until soft. Add the lemon juice to the pan and stir to combine. Transfer the mixture to a bowl.

Melt the remaining butter in the same frying pan, add the salmon fillet, and cook for 2 minutes on each side to brown it. Transfer to a plate and allow to cool slightly.

Lightly grease a baking sheet. Roll out half the pastry to a rectangle measuring 12 x 16 inches and place on the baking sheet. Spread the rice mixture onto the pastry, leaving a 1 1/4-inch border all the way around. Top with the piece of salmon and then add the mushroom mixture. Mold the layers to fit the shape of the salmon fillet.

Roll out the remaining pastry to approximately 13 x 17 inches and carefully place over the filling. Press the edges of the pastry together, trim the edges to a neat rectangle, and crimp to seal. Decorate with pastry shapes, if desired, then refrigerate for 30 minutes. Meanwhile, preheat the oven to 415°F. Brush the pastry with the lightly beaten egg and make four slits in the top to allow the steam to escape. Bake for 15 minutes, then reduce the heat to 350°F and bake for an additional 15–20 minutes or until the top is golden brown.

Fish substitution—ocean trout, trout

Roll out half the pastry to a 12 x 16-inch rectangle

Top the pastry with the rice mixture and the fish fillet

sardine ripiene

TO MAKE A SARDINE DISH MEMORABLE, THE FISH MUST BE REALLY FRESH; SARDINES, LIKE MACKEREL, DO NOT LAST LONG OUT OF THE WATER. WHOLE SARDINES WILL LOOK NEATER, AS YOU CAN JUST FOLD THE FISH IN HALF. IF YOU CAN ONLY GET FILLETS, TRY TO GET THEM WITH THEIR TAILS ON, AS THESE WILL LOOK MORE ATTRACTIVE.

sardines	8 medium, butterflied (heads removed, tails left on)
olive oil	1/4 cup
onion	1 small, thinly sliced
fennel bulb	1, thinly sliced
pine nuts	1/3 cup
Italian parsley	1/4 cup roughly chopped
fresh bread crumbs	1/4 cup
garlic	1 large clove, crushed
lemon juice	2 tablespoons
extra-virgin olive oil	to serve
lemon wedges	to serve

Rinse the sardines in cold water and drain on paper towels. Leave in the refrigerator until needed.

Preheat the oven to 400°F. To prepare the stuffing, heat the olive oil in a frying pan and add the onion, fennel, and pine nuts. Cook over moderately high heat until soft and light brown, stirring frequently. Mix 1 tablespoon of the parsley with 1 tablespoon of bread crumbs and set aside. Add the garlic and remaining bread crumbs to the pan and cook for a few minutes more. Add the rest of the parsley, season, and set aside. The stuffing mix can be made in advance and kept in the refrigerator, but should be brought back to room temperature before cooking.

Drizzle a little olive oil in an ovenproof dish in which eight sardines can fit in a single layer. Arrange the fish in the dish, skin side down, and season with salt and pepper. Spread the stuffing over the sardines and fold over to encase. If you are using fillets, spread half the fillets with stuffing, then place the other fillets on top, skin side up, tail to tail like a sandwich. Season again and sprinkle with the parsley and bread crumb mixture. Drizzle with the lemon juice and a little extra-virgin olive oil.

Bake for 5–10 minutes, depending on the size of the sardines. If the filling is still warm, the sardines will cook more quickly. Serve immediately or at room temperature with lemon wedges.

To butterfly sardines, first scale, gut, and clean them

The next step is to cut along the back, then remove the head

Finally, lift the backbone away from the flesh

three ways with pâté

THESE RECIPES USE DIFFERENT TYPES OF SMOKED FISH. SMOKED FOODS ARE FIRST TREATED WITH EITHER BRINE OR DRY SALT, THEN SMOKED OVER SMOLDERING SAWDUST. THE WOOD USED HELPS DETERMINE THE FLAVOR OF THE FINISHED PRODUCT. THERE ARE TWO METHODS OF SMOKING: COLD SMOKING FLAVORS THE FOOD WITHOUT COOKING IT; SUCH FOODS GENERALLY NEED TO BE COOKED BEFORE THEY ARE EATEN, WITH SMOKED SALMON BEING AN EXCEPTION. HOT SMOKING COOKS THE FOOD WHILE ALSO IMPARTING A DELICIOUS SMOKY FLAVOR.

smoked trout pâté

Skin 2 whole smoked trout, remove the heads, then lift the flesh off the bones. Alternatively, use 4 skinless smoked trout fillets. Flake the flesh and put in a bowl or food processor. Either mash the flesh with a fork or briefly blend until it is broken up, but still with plenty of texture. Beat 3/4 cup cream cheese with a wooden spoon until soft. Add the smoked trout flesh and mix together well. Stir in 2 tablespoons finely chopped dill and the juice of half a lemon. Season with salt, freshly ground black pepper, and a pinch of cayenne pepper. Chill the pâté until you need it, but bring it to room temperature before serving. Serve with toasted slices of baguette, melba toast, or triangles of wheat toast with the crusts removed. Provide extra lemon wedges to squeeze over. Serves 6.

smoked salmon pâté

Put 2 tablespoons rinsed, dried, and roughly chopped capers and 1 seeded and finely chopped small red chili in a food processor. Add 3 1/2 ounces smoked salmon (trimmings are fine) and blend for about 10 seconds. Add 3/4 cup mascarpone cheese and blend until smooth. Add 3–4 tablespoons milk, depending on how thick the pâté is, and blend again. Transfer to a bowl and add 1 tablespoon finely chopped Italian parsley and 1–2 tablespoons lemon juice to taste. Season with salt and freshly ground black pepper and refrigerate until needed. Serve with melba toast or triangles of wheat toast with the crusts removed. Serves 4–6.

smoked mackerel pâté

Remove the skin from 8 ounces peppered, smoked mackerel fillets (about 2 fillets). Put them in a bowl and mash with a fork. Add 1/3 cup sour cream, 1 tablespoon creamed horseradish, and 2 tablespoons lime juice. Mix everything together well, season with a little salt if needed, then refrigerate until ready to use. Serve with melba toast or triangles of wheat toast with the crusts removed. This also makes a great sandwich filling with watercress. Serves 4–6.

caruru .... serves 4

THIS RICH AND CREAMY BRAZILIAN STEW HAS AN AFRICAN INFLUENCE. IT IS TRADITIONALLY SERVED WITH A SPICY PEPPER AND LEMON SAUCE CONSISTING OF TABASCO PEPPERS, ONIONS, GARLIC, AND LEMON JUICE.

tomatoes	3 large
dried shrimp	1 tablespoon
oil	3 tablespoons
onion	1, chopped
green bell pepper	1 small, seeded and chopped
green chili	1, finely chopped
garlic	3 cloves, crushed
crunchy peanut butter	3 tablespoons
coconut milk	$1^2/_3$ cups
okra	$1^1/_4$ cups small, topped and tailed
paprika	$1/_2$ teaspoon
cod fillet	1 pound, 5 ounces, skinless
cilantro	3 tablespoons chopped

Score a cross in the base of each tomato. Plunge into boiling water for 20 seconds, then drain and peel the skin away from the cross. Chop the tomatoes, discarding the cores and seeds.

Put the dried shrimp in a small bowl, cover with boiling water, and leave to soak for 10 minutes, then drain.

Heat the oil in a deep-sided frying pan. Add the onion and green bell pepper and cook for 5 minutes, stirring occasionally. Add the chili and garlic and cook for an additional 2 minutes, stirring. Add the chopped tomato and its juices, peanut butter, coconut milk, okra, paprika, and dried shrimp. Bring the mixture to a boil, then reduce the heat to medium and simmer for 12–15 minutes or until the okra are tender.

Meanwhile, cut the cod into large chunks. Add the fish to the pan, stir, and simmer gently to cook. Test after 3 minutes; if the cod flakes easily, it is ready. Season and sprinkle the cilantro over the top.

Fish substitution—bream, bass, shrimp

Note: Dried shrimp are available from stores selling Asian or South American and Caribbean produce. You may need to soak the dried shrimp for more than 10 minutes if they are very hard.

Chop the peeled tomatoes, discarding the cores and seeds

Cover the dried shrimp with boiling water and leave to soak

Add the tomato, peanut butter, coconut milk, okra, and shrimp

redfish in corn husks with asparagus and red bell pepper dressing . . . . serves 6

PREPARED CORN HUSKS ARE AVAILABLE FOR MAKING TAMALES. IF PREPARING YOUR OWN, CUT OFF THE BASE AND POINTS OF THE HUSKS. POUR BOILING WATER OVER THE HUSKS AND LET SOAK FOR SEVERAL HOURS OR UNTIL PLIABLE. DRAIN AND DRY THEM WELL BEFORE FILLING THEM, OR USE BAKING PAPER OR FOIL INSTEAD.

red bell pepper dressing

red bell pepper	1
extra-virgin olive oil	2 tablespoons
garlic	1 small clove, crushed
lemon juice	1 tablespoon
basil	1 tablespoon chopped
pine nuts	1 tablespoon
small black olives	1/2 cup
redfish	6 small, scaled and gutted
lemon thyme	12 sprigs
lemon	1, sliced
garlic	2 cloves, sliced
corn husks	12 large
olive oil	for drizzling
fresh asparagus	2 bunches, trimmed
lemon wedges	for serving

To make the red bell pepper dressing, cut the bell pepper into large pieces. Place, skin side up, under a hot broiler until the skin blackens and blisters. (Alternatively, hold the bell pepper over the gas flame of your stove until the skin blackens.) Put the bell pepper in a plastic bag, seal the bag, and allow the bell pepper to cool before peeling away the skin and finely dicing the flesh.

In a small bowl, whisk together the extra-virgin olive oil, garlic, lemon juice, and basil. Add the bell pepper, pine nuts, and olives.

Wash the fish and pat dry inside and out with paper towels. Fill each fish cavity with thyme, lemon, and garlic, then place each fish in a corn husk. Drizzle with oil and sprinkle with freshly ground black pepper, then top each fish with another husk. Tie each end of the husks with string to enclose.

Preheat the barbecue or a coal fire to high. Put the parcels on the barbecue or coals and cook for 6–8 minutes or until the fish is cooked and flakes easily when tested with a knife. Turn the parcels once during the cooking. A few minutes after you have started cooking the fish, brush the asparagus with oil and add to the barbecue or coals. Cook, turning occasionally, for 3–4 minutes or until tender. Pour the dressing over the asparagus and serve with the fish. Discard the husks before eating.

Fish substitution—red mullet

Fill the cavity of each fish with thyme, lemon, and garlic

Place each fish in a corn husk, drizzle with oil, and season

Cook on a barbecue or over coals, turning once

the perfect fish stock

A good homemade fish stock makes a huge difference to fish-based soups, sauces, and stews, and is the simplest of all stocks to make. It is also quick to make—in fact, cooking it too long will produce a bitter stock. Fish stock is made by simmering together the uncooked fish bones and heads and/or the shells of crustaceans with water, vegetables, and a few aromatics such as peppercorns and herbs. To make a decent amount of stock, quite a few bones are needed; the easiest way to get them is to ask a fishmonger for leftover bones after the fish has been filleted (or, fillet the fish yourself and retain the bones). Store the bones in the freezer until you have enough. It is important to avoid oily fish such as herring and mackerel.

To make fish stock, put about 2 pounds, 4 ounces fish bones, heads, and trimmings (but not any innards), and crustacean shells in a large saucepan. Add 1 roughly chopped onion, 1 thickly sliced carrot, a few peppercorns, 1 bay leaf, and some parsley stalks (not the leaves) if you have any. Cover with about 8 cups water and bring to a boil. Reduce to a simmer and cook uncovered for 20 minutes, skimming off any film that comes to the surface. Strain, then leave to cool. Refrigerate until needed, removing any fat that forms on the surface. Store in the refrigerator for up to 3 days or freeze for up to 6 months.

If freezer space is limited, return the strained stock to a clean saucepan and boil vigorously until the stock is reduced by two-thirds to three-fourths. Leave to cool, then pour into ice-cube trays and freeze. Once frozen, the cubes can then be transferred to freezer bags. When using the concentrated stock cubes, remember to add water to the dish to return the stock to its original strength.

russian fish pies with mushrooms and sour cream .... serves 4

PIES KNOWN AS PIROGI ARE VERY POPULAR IN RUSSIA. THEY ARE USUALLY LARGE AND RECTANGULAR, BUT THIS RECIPE MAKES INDIVIDUAL CRESCENT-SHAPED PIES. THE FILLINGS MAY BE SAVORY OR SWEET. FISH PIROGI ARE TRADITIONALLY MADE WITH STURGEON, BUT ANY FIRM WHITE FISH MAY BE USED.

pastry

all-purpose flour	2 1/3 cups
salt	a pinch
butter	3/4 cup, chilled and cubed
egg yolks	3 large
iced water	as needed

filling

long-grain white rice	1/3 cup
firm white fish fillet	1 pound, skinless
butter	1/4 cup
mushrooms	3 cups, sliced
sour cream	3/4 cup
lemon juice	1 tablespoon
Italian parsley	3 tablespoons chopped

To make the pastry, sieve the flour with a generous pinch of salt into a large bowl. Rub the butter into the flour until fine crumbs form. Lightly beat two of the egg yolks and stir into the flour mixture with a little iced water. Mix together, adding more water if necessary to bring the dough together. Wrap the dough in plastic wrap and refrigerate for at least 30 minutes.

To make the filling, put the rice in a small saucepan with 1/2 cup boiling water and a pinch of salt. Bring to a boil, then reduce the heat to medium-low and cook covered with a tight-fitting lid for 15 minutes. Add an additional 1–2 tablespoons boiling water if the rice begins to dry out. Allow to cool.

Chop the fish coarsely. Melt the butter in a large frying pan and when hot, add the mushrooms. Cook for 4–5 minutes or until soft. Add the fish and cook, stirring occasionally, for 4–5 minutes or until the fish is opaque. Remove the pan from the heat and stir in the cooked rice, sour cream, lemon juice, and parsley. Season with salt and freshly ground black pepper and set aside until cold. Preheat the oven to 375°F.

Roll the pastry out on a floured work surface to a thickness of 1/8 inch. Cut out 8 or 10 circles, each 4 1/2 inches in diameter. Put a tablespoon of filling on each circle, leaving a border around the edges, and fold the pastry in half to form a crescent shape. Press the edges together to seal. Cut two slits in the top of each pie to allow steam to escape. Transfer the pies to a large oiled and floured baking sheet.

Mix the remaining egg yolk with a teaspoon of water and use to brush the edges of the pastry. Fold the pastry in half, seal the pocket, and brush the outside with the egg yolk. Make two small cuts in the top for steam holes. Bake in the preheated oven for 30–35 minutes or until the pastry is golden.

steamed snapper with asian flavors

....serves 2

THERE ARE VARIOUS SPECIES OF FISH KNOWN AS SNAPPERS IN CARIBBEAN, PACIFIC, AND ASIAN WATERS. MOST MAKE VERY FINE EATING. AS THEY AGE, SOME SPECIES DEVELOP A DISTINCTIVE BULGE ABOVE THE EYES. LEMONGRASS, CILANTRO, AND GINGER ADD A PIQUANT ASIAN TOUCH TO THIS DISH.

whole snapper	1, about 1 pound, 12 ounces (scaled, gutted, and fins removed)
lemongrass	3 stems
cilantro leaves	a handful
fresh ginger	1¼-inch piece, peeled and julienned
garlic	1 large clove, peeled and cut into thin slivers
soy sauce	2 tablespoons
oil	¼ cup
fish sauce	1 tablespoon
red chili	1 small, seeded and finely diced
stir-fried Asian greens	to serve

Score the fish with diagonal cuts on both sides. Cut each lemongrass stem into three and lightly squash each piece with the end of the handle of a large knife. Put half of the lemongrass in the middle of a large piece of foil and lay the fish on top. Put the remaining lemongrass and half the cilantro inside the cavity of the fish.

Mix the ginger, garlic, soy sauce, oil, fish sauce, and chili together in a bowl. Drizzle the mixture over the fish and sprinkle with the remaining cilantro leaves.

Enclose the fish in the foil and place in a bamboo or metal steamer over a large saucepan of simmering water. Steam for 25 minutes or until the flesh of the fish is opaque and white. Transfer the foil package to a large serving plate and open at the table. Serve the fish with stir-fried Asian greens and steamed rice.

Fish substitution—coral trout, sea bass, red emperor

Fresh cilantro is thought to be the world's most commonly used herb. Every part can be used: roots, stems, leaves, and seeds. Different cuisines favor different parts: the seeds figure highly in European cooking, the roots are pounded for use in Thai curry pastes, and the fresh leaves are used liberally in Southeast Asian and Latin American cooking. From India to Indonesia, the seeds are a vital part of curry pastes and spice mixes. In most Asian cooking, cilantro leaves and roots are a key component in fish and shellfish dishes, due to the herb's aromatic flavor and natural affinity with such ingredients as ginger, chilies, lemongrass, and lime juice.

otak-otak . . . . makes 14

THESE SPICY FISH CAKES ARE SEEN IN THE MARKETS OF SINGAPORE, COOKING OVER HOT COALS OR UNDER A BROILER, AND ARE A POPULAR LUNCHTIME SNACK. THE PARCELS CAN BE UNWRAPPED AND THE STEAMING CONTENTS EATEN IMMEDIATELY, OR CHILLED AND EATEN AS A LIGHT SNACK WHEN COLD.

grouper fillets	1 pound, skinless and boned
dried red chilies	2 small
banana leaf	14 pieces, measuring 4¹/₂ x 6¹/₄ inches
lemongrass	1 stem, cut into three pieces
onion	1 small, peeled and cut in half
garlic	1 large clove, peeled
ground turmeric	a generous pinch
palm sugar	1 teaspoon grated (soft brown sugar can be substituted)
salt	a generous pinch
ground coriander	1 teaspoon
shrimp paste (balacan)	1 teaspoon
candlenuts, unsalted macadamia nuts, or peanuts	1 tablespoon
mint	1 tablespoon chopped
cilantro	1 tablespoon chopped
coconut milk	¹/₄ cup

Cut the fillets into chunks. Cover and refrigerate until required.

Put the dried chilies in a small bowl, cover with boiling water, and leave to soak. Put 14 toothpicks in a bowl and cover with cold water to soak.

If the banana leaf has been frozen, it will be soft when thawed, but if fresh—and tough—it can be softened by blanching in boiling water for a minute, then draining and refreshing in cold water. Put the fish in a food processor and blend to a thick purée. Transfer to a mixing bowl. Drain the chilies, removing any stalks still attached, and put in the processor with the lemongrass, onion, garlic, turmeric, sugar, salt, ground coriander, shrimp paste, nuts, mint, cilantro, and coconut milk. Blend to a paste. Add the paste to the fish and mix to combine.

Drain the toothpicks. Put about 2 tablespoons of mixture in the middle of each piece of banana leaf. Enclose the filling by folding the shorter sides of the rectangle into the middle so that they overlap. Fold the two protruding ends in to make a small package. Secure the ends with a toothpick.

Preheat the broiler or barbecue. Either put the parcels, smooth side up, on a baking sheet and broil 4 inches from the element for 5 minutes, or put the parcels, smooth side down, on the barbecue and cook for 5 minutes. The parcels are ready when the banana leaf has lightly browned and the parcels are hot in the middle (open them to check this). Eat warm or cold.

Fish substitution—hapuka, blue warehou, halibut, haddock, snapper

If using fresh banana leaf, blanch first, then drain and refresh

Enclose the filling in the banana leaf and secure with a toothpick

crispy fried fish
with chili and cucumber .... serves 2

DEEP-FRYING WHOLE FISH UNTIL GOLDEN AND CRISP IS AN ASIAN TECHNIQUE. TURNING THE FISH IS LESS TRICKY IF YOU USE TWO SPIDERS, TOOLS THAT HAVE SEVERAL METAL SEGMENTS THAT FAN OUT, GIVING A LARGE SURFACE AREA AND ALLOWING YOU TO MANEUVER A WHOLE FISH WHILE KEEPING IT INTACT.

whole pomfret	1 pound, 2 ounces, head intact, scaled and gutted
oil	¼ cup
red Asian shallots	4, or 1 small onion, thinly sliced
garlic	1 clove, finely chopped
fresh ginger	1 teaspoon grated
red chilies	3 small, seeded and finely chopped
palm sugar	2 tablespoons, grated (soft brown sugar can be substituted)
tamarind purée	1 tablespoon
lime	zest and juice of 1
fish sauce	2 tablespoons
short cucumber	1 large, peeled and cut into thin batons
oil	for deep-frying
cilantro leaves	1 tablespoon chopped

Score diagonal cuts on both sides of the fish.

Heat the oil in a wok or sauté pan. When the oil is just beginning to smoke, add the shallots or onion, stir, and cook for 2 minutes or until they begin to soften and color. Add the garlic, ginger, and chilies, and cook for an additional minute or until lightly golden and crisp. Combine the sugar, tamarind, lime juice, and fish sauce together, and add to the mixture. Allow to bubble for 30 seconds or until the sauce thickens slightly. Stir in the cucumber and remove from the heat. Transfer the sauce to a small saucepan and set aside.

Clean the wok or pan and add oil to a depth of 1 inch. Heat to 350°F or until a cube of white bread dropped into the oil browns in 15 seconds. Gently lower the fish into the oil and cook for 4–5 minutes or until golden and crisp. Make sure the skin does not stick to the wok by moving the fish to and fro as you lower it in. Turn once during cooking, and spoon the hot oil over the fish as it cooks. Meanwhile, gently reheat the sauce. Drain the fish on paper towels. To serve, drizzle the sauce over the fish, then sprinkle with lime zest and cilantro.

Fish substitution—snapper, sea bass, bream

Once the oil begins to smoke, add the shallots

Gently lower the fish into the oil and cook until golden and crisp

Turn the fish once and spoon hot oil over it as it cooks

goan fish curry

serves 4

THE FOOD OF GOA, ON INDIA'S SOUTHWEST COAST, HAS BEEN INFLUENCED BY THE PORTUGUESE, WHO LIVED IN THE AREA FOR 500 YEARS AND INTRODUCED THE NOW-UBIQUITOUS CHILI. COCONUT, GARLIC, GINGER, AND SOURING AGENTS SUCH AS TAMARIND ARE ALSO COMMON IN THE REGION'S CUISINE.

cardamom pods	4
coriander seeds	1 teaspoon
yellow mustard seeds	2 teaspoons
shredded coconut	2 tablespoons
oil	1/4 cup
onion	1 large, chopped
garlic	2 cloves, finely chopped
green chilies	3 small, seeded and finely chopped
fresh ginger	1 tablespoon grated
ground turmeric	1/2 teaspoon
nutmeg	a pinch of freshly grated
cloves	4
tamarind purée	2 tablespoons
curry leaves	6
cinnamon sticks	2
coconut milk	3 1/4 cups
pomfret, flounder, or sole fillets	1 pound, 5 ounces, skinless and cut into strips
small raw shrimp	12, peeled and deveined
cilantro leaves	to garnish, optional

Lightly crush the cardamom pods until the pods split, then remove the seeds from the pods and put in a small frying pan with the coriander seeds. Dry-fry until fragrant and the seeds begin to jump. Remove from the heat and tip into a mortar and pestle or spice grinder. Grind the seeds to a powder.

Tip the mustard seeds into the frying pan with the coconut and toast together until the seeds begin to pop and the coconut turns light golden. Remove from the heat and set aside.

Heat the oil in a medium saucepan and add the onion. Cook for 4–5 minutes or until the onions soften. Add the garlic, chili, ginger, turmeric, and nutmeg, and cook for an additional minute. Tip in the ground spices, the toasted coconut and mustard seeds, the cloves, tamarind, curry leaves, cinnamon sticks, and coconut milk. Stir well and heat to just below boiling point, then reduce the heat and simmer uncovered for 10 minutes or until slightly thickened. Add the fish and shrimp and poach for 5 minutes or until the fish is opaque and the shrimp are pale pink.

Cardamom is a sweet, aromatic spice, used in both sweet and savory dishes. In Africa, it is added to coffee and spice mixes such as the Moroccan ras el hanout; Scandinavian cooks flavor cookies with its mild sweetness; and in India, the seeds are used whole or ground to flavor curries, rice dishes, and milk desserts. In Goan cuisine, cardamom is most often seen in the spicy fish dishes that are at the heart of the region's cooking. During its colonial period, Goa was an important trading stop for Portugal, and cardamom was one of its most valuable commodities. Buy the seeds still in the pod, as they lose their flavor quickly once rid of the protective shell.

baked coral trout and fennel . . . . serves 2

FENNEL MAKES A WONDERFULLY AROMATIC COMPLEMENT FOR FISH. THE FINE, FEATHERY LEAVES CAN BE SNIPPED LIKE AN HERB AND USED TO FLAVOR FISH. THE BULB MAY BE EATEN RAW LIKE CELERY, OR BRAISED OR SAUTÉED AND ADDED TO RECIPES. ALL PARTS HAVE A DELICATE FLAVOR SIMILAR TO ANISEED.

fennel bulbs	2 small, about 9$\frac{1}{2}$ ounces each
butter	2 tablespoons
olive oil	2 tablespoons
onion	1, chopped
garlic	1 clove, crushed
coral trout	1, gutted and scaled
	(about 1 pound, 12 ounces to
	2 pounds, 4 ounces after cleaning)
extra-virgin olive oil	for brushing
lemon	1, quartered
oregano	2 teaspoons chopped
lemon wedges	to serve

Preheat the oven to 375°F and grease a large, shallow ovenproof dish. Finely slice the fennel bulbs, reserving the green fronds.

Heat the butter and olive oil in a large frying pan and gently cook the fennel, onion, and garlic for 12–15 minutes or until softened but not browned. Season with salt and pepper.

Stuff the fish with a heaping tablespoon of the cooked fennel mixture and a quarter of the fennel fronds. Brush with extra-virgin olive oil, squeeze the lemon over, and season well.

Put the remaining fennel fronds and cooked fennel into the dish and sprinkle with half of the oregano. Arrange the fish on top of the fennel. Sprinkle the remaining oregano over the fish and cover the dish loosely with foil. Bake for 25 minutes or until just cooked through. Serve with lemon wedges and small boiled potatoes, and top with some of the cooked fennel mixture.

Fish substitution—snapper

Coral trout (also known as coral cod) is not related to true trouts or cods, but is instead a species of grouper. Its coloration is striking; the body is a pink-orange with blue spots. These fish are found in Indo-Pacific waters and, like all groupers, can grow to enormous sizes, but it is the smaller specimens that make the best eating. The firm, flaky flesh lends itself well to a variety of cooking methods.

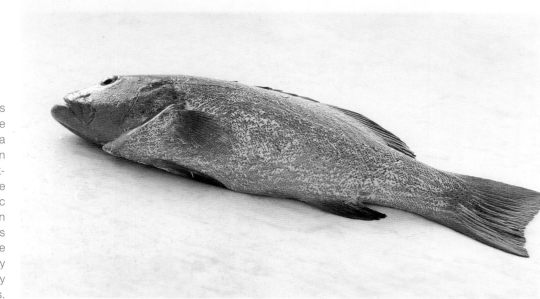

three ways with flatfish

FLATFISH INCLUDE FLOUNDER, SOLE, HALIBUT, DAB, AND TURBOT. STRICTLY SPEAKING, THE TERM APPLIES TO ONE ZOOLOGICAL ORDER OF MOSTLY AMBUSH-FEEDING FISH THAT LIE ON THEIR SIDES ON THE SEABED, AND WHOSE HEADS HAVE BECOME TWISTED AROUND SO THAT BOTH EYES ARE NOW ON THE TOP SIDE. HOWEVER, SOME NARROW FISH THAT SWIM UPRIGHT, SUCH AS JOHN DORY AND POMFRET, ARE ALSO SOMETIMES CALLED FLATFISH, AND CAN BE SUBSTITUTED FOR TRUE FLATFISH.

john dory with pea purée

Chop 1 onion and finely chop 2 bacon slices (total weight about 3 ounces). Heat 1 tablespoon olive oil in a medium saucepan and fry the onion and bacon for 4–5 minutes. Stir in 1¾ cups frozen peas, ¾ cup vegetable or chicken stock, and 1 mint sprig. Bring to a boil, then simmer for about 10 minutes. Allow to cool slightly, discard the mint sprig, and transfer to a blender or food processor. Process until roughly puréed; the mixture should not be smooth. Return to the clean saucepan, stir in 2 tablespoons heavy cream, season, and gently reheat. Meanwhile, wash and pat dry four 6-ounce skinless John Dory fillets. Dust lightly in seasoned flour and fry in 1 tablespoon melted butter for about 3 minutes, two at a time if necessary. Turn and cook for 1–2 minutes on the other side or until golden brown. Serve the fillets on a bed of pea purée. Serves 4.

turbot with creamy mushroom sauce

Preheat the oven to 250°F and warm four plates. Put 1 tablespoon oil and a small pat of butter in a large frying pan over high heat. Once the butter is bubbling, add four 6-ounce skinless turbot or other flatfish fillets (you may need to add them two at a time). Leave for 3 minutes, then turn over and cook for 1–2 minutes or until just cooked through. Transfer the fillets to the oven to keep warm. Add an additional tablespoon of oil to the pan and add 2 cups finely chopped Swiss brown mushrooms. Fry for 2 minutes or until softened. Add 1 cup heavy cream. Cook until heated through. Remove from the heat, stir in 2 tablespoons chopped chives, and season with salt and freshly ground black pepper. Spoon over the fish and serve immediately, accompanied by lemon wedges. Serves 4.

warm turbot salad with shaved fennel

Steam four 6-ounce skinless turbot fillets for about 5 minutes over simmering water, until just cooked. Set aside to cool slightly. Meanwhile, combine ⅓ cup olive oil and 2 tablespoons sherry vinegar. Trim and very thinly slice 1 baby fennel and put in a bowl with half the oil and vinegar. Toss together. Arrange 5 cups mixed salad leaves on four serving plates and top with the fennel and turbot. Sprinkle with a handful of mint leaves and drizzle over the remaining dressing. Serves 4.

john dory with pea purée

sole à la meunière .... serves 4

OF THE MANY SPECIES OF SOLE, THE MOST PRIZED IS THE SPECIES *SOLEA SOLEA*. IT IS OFTEN CALLED DOVER SOLE TO DISTINGUISH IT FROM THE UNRELATED LEMON SOLE. THE SIMPLE LEMON AND BUTTER SAUCE OF THIS CLASSIC RECIPE COMPLEMENTS THE SOLE'S FIRM WHITE FLESH AND DELICATE FLAVOR.

whole dover sole	4, gutted, with dark skin removed
all-purpose flour	1/4 cup
salt	to taste
ground white pepper	to taste
clarified butter	3/4 cup (see note)
lemon juice	2 tablespoons
Italian parsley	4 tablespoons chopped
lemon wedges	to serve
steamed greens	to serve

Pat the fish dry with paper towels. Season the flour with salt and freshly ground white pepper. Cut away the fine bones and frill of skin from around the edge of the fish, remove the heads if you like, and dust lightly with the flour. Heat three quarters of the butter in a frying pan large enough to fit all four fish, or cook the fish in two batches, using half the amount of butter for each batch.

Put the fish in the pan, skinless side up, and cook for 4 minutes or until golden. Carefully turn over and cook for an additional 4 minutes or until the fish is cooked through (the flesh will feel firm when done). Put the fish, skinless side up, on warm plates, drizzle with the lemon juice, and sprinkle with the parsley. Add the remaining butter to the pan and heat until it browns, but do not let it get too brown or the sauce will taste burned. Pour over the fish (it will foam as it mixes with the lemon juice) and serve with lemon wedges and steamed greens.

Fish substitution—sole fillets

Note: Clarified butter has a higher burning point than other butters because it doesn't contain any milk solids. To clarify butter, gently heat unsalted butter in a saucepan until liquid; do not stir. Leave until the white milk solids settle to the bottom. Use a spoon to skim off any foam, then strain off the golden liquid, leaving the white solids behind. Refrigerate the liquid.

Cut away the fine bones and frill of skin from the edge of the fish

Lightly dust the fish with the seasoned flour

Put the fish in the pan, skinless side up, and cook until golden

escabeche . . . . serves 2

ESCABECHE IS A WAY OF PRESERVING FISH. THE FISH IS FIRST FRIED AND THEN MARINATED OVERNIGHT IN A PICKLING SOLUTION. ORIGINALLY SPANISH, THE RECIPE HAS SPREAD TO MANY OTHER PLACES. THIS RECIPE USES CINNAMON, NUTMEG, AND CITRUS JUICES, FLAVORS THAT ARE OFTEN FOUND IN SOUTH AFRICAN DISHES.

sea bass or snook fillet	1 pound, skinless
cod or barracuda fillet	1 pound, skinless
all-purpose flour	1 cup
vegetable oil	1/2 cup
onion	1 medium, finely sliced into rings
garlic	1 large clove, finely chopped
white wine vinegar	3/4 cup
orange juice	2 tablespoons
lemon juice	2 tablespoons
orange zest	2 teaspoons
lemon zest	2 teaspoons
superfine sugar	2 tablespoons
ground cinnamon	2 teaspoons
ground nutmeg	2 teaspoons
turmeric	1/4 teaspoon
paprika	1/4 teaspoon

Cut the fish fillets into strips measuring approximately 4 1/2 x 1 1/4 inches. Put the flour onto a plate and season with salt and pepper. Dip the fish in the seasoned flour.

Heat 3 tablespoons of the oil in a frying pan until hot and cook the fish for 2 minutes on each side or until lightly golden and crisp. You will need to cook in batches, so add an additional tablespoon of oil if necessary. Drain the cooked fish on crumpled paper towels, then arrange in a single layer on a serving dish or platter.

Wipe out the pan and add the remaining oil. When hot, add the onion and cook, stirring, over low heat for 4–5 minutes or until soft. Add the garlic and cook, stirring, for 2 minutes. Stir in the vinegar, juices, zests, sugar, cinnamon, nutmeg, turmeric, paprika, and 1/3 cup water. Bring to a boil, simmer for 5 minutes, then pour over the fish. Allow to cool, then cover and refrigerate overnight. Once cooked and marinated, the fish will keep for up to a week in the refrigerator. Eat at room temperature.

Fish substitution—snapper, halibut, bream

Citrus zest—the thin, colored outer layer of the rind—contains aromatic essential oils, which are rich in flavor. These oils release their flavor most readily when combined with fats, which is why citrus zests are often creamed with butter and sugar in baked goods such as cakes and cookies. Zests can also be infused in warm liquids or syrups to flavor them, and the liquid then added to the recipe. The zest can be grated, removed in fine scrolls with a special tool called a zester, or be pared off in wider strips with a vegetable peeler and then sliced more finely if desired. Take care to remove and use the zest only, not the white pith beneath, which is bitter.

cullen skink

THIS SCOTTISH SOUP TRADITIONALLY INCLUDES FINNAN HADDOCK, OR "FINNAN HADDIE," THE FAMOUS SMOKED HADDOCK FROM THE VILLAGE OF FINDON, NEAR ABERDEEN. THE SMOKED FISH GIVES THE SOUP A DELICIOUS DEPTH OF FLAVOR AND THE THICK TEXTURE MAKES IT A ROBUST WINTER WARMER.

smoked haddock (preferably Finnan haddock)	1 pound, 5 ounces
milk	5 cups
butter	1 tablespoon
smoked bacon	3 1/2 ounces, diced
onion	1 large, chopped
waxy potatoes (e.g., red)	1 pound, 2 ounces, peeled and cut into small chunks
light cream	1/4 cup
chives	3 tablespoons chopped

Put the haddock in a sauté pan or deep-frying pan and pour the milk over the top. Bring the liquid to a boil, then reduce to a simmer, cover, and poach gently for 10 minutes. When ready, the fish should be flaky when tested with the point of a sharp knife. Drain, reserving the milk. Flake the haddock into small pieces, discarding any skin and bones. Set aside.

Meanwhile, melt the butter in a large saucepan and when foaming, add the bacon and onion. Cook on medium–low heat for 10 minutes or until the onion has softened and is translucent. Add the potatoes and the reserved milk. Bring to a boil and simmer covered for 15–20 minutes or until the potatoes are cooked. Stir in the haddock and cream, season to taste with salt and pepper, and bring back to a gentle simmer. Sprinkle with the chopped chives before serving.

Fish substitution—smoked cod

Put the haddock in the pan and cover it with the milk

Test the fish with the point of a knife to see if it is cooked

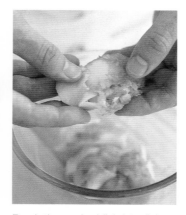

Break the cooked fish into flakes, discarding the skin and bones

hot and sour fish stew .... serves 4

COMBINATIONS OF HOT AND SOUR INGREDIENTS—SUCH AS FRESH CHILIES, GARLIC, SUGAR, LIME JUICE, AND VINEGAR OR TAMARIND—ARE OFTEN FOUND IN SOUTHEAST ASIAN COOKING.

spice paste

lemongrass	2 stems, white part only, cut into three pieces
ground turmeric	1 teaspoon
fresh galangal or ginger	1 teaspoon grated
red chilies	3 small
garlic	1 large clove, peeled
red Asian shallots	4, peeled
shrimp paste	1 teaspoon
oil	1/4 cup
red bell pepper	1/2 small, thinly sliced into strips
tamarind purée or lemon juice	3 tablespoons
fish sauce	1 tablespoon
palm sugar	2 teaspoons, grated (soft brown sugar can be substituted)
canned sliced bamboo shoots	1 3/4 cups, drained
pomfret fillets	1 pound, 2 ounces skinless, cut into bite-sized pieces
cilantro leaves	2 tablespoons chopped
mint	1 tablespoon chopped
steamed rice	to serve

To make the spice paste, put all the ingredients in a food processor and process to a paste. Alternatively, finely chop all the ingredients and mix together by hand.

Heat the oil in a large saucepan and add the spice paste. Cook for 10 minutes, stirring. Add the bell pepper strips and cook for an additional minute. Add 3 cups water, the tamarind, fish sauce, sugar, and 1/2 teaspoon salt, and bring to a boil. Reduce the heat to low and simmer for 5 minutes, then add the bamboo shoots and fish pieces and poach the fish gently for 3–4 minutes or until opaque. Stir in the cilantro and mint and serve over plenty of steamed rice.

Fish substitution—lemon sole (lemon fish), flounder, sea bass, John Dory

Finely process the spice paste ingredients in a food processor

Add the bamboo shoots and fish pieces to the mixture

roasted blue-eye cod with lentil salad........... serves 4

BLUE-EYE COD IS COMMONLY FOUND IN THE COLD SEAS OFF THE SOUTH ISLAND OF NEW ZEALAND, WHERE IT IS AVAILABLE AND EATEN ALL YEAR. ITS FIRM WHITE FLESH IS HIGHLY REGARDED AND, LIKE OTHER TYPES OF COD, ITS THICKNESS SUITS ROASTING AT A HIGH TEMPERATURE.

puy lentils	1 cup
pine nuts	1/3 cup
olive oil	1/3 cup
red bell pepper	1, seeded and cut into thin strips
orange bell pepper	1, seeded and cut into thin strips
blue-eye cod	4 thick fillets, skinless
lemon juice	1 tablespoon
red onion	1 small, finely diced
balsamic vinegar	1/4 cup
basil	2 tablespoons shredded

Put the lentils in a saucepan, cover with water, and bring to a boil over high heat. Boil for 5 minutes, then reduce the heat to medium and continue to cook uncovered for 15–20 minutes or until the lentils are tender. You may need to top the lentils with boiling water as they cook. Drain and rinse under warm water.

Meanwhile, preheat the oven to 425°F. Place the pine nuts in a frying pan and toast over low–medium heat until golden brown, shaking occasionally. Transfer to a plate.

Heat 1 tablespoon of the olive oil in the frying pan and, when hot, add the strips of bell pepper. Stirring occasionally, cook for 5–7 minutes over medium heat or until tender when tested with the point of a small knife. Remove from the heat.

Put the fish in a roasting pan, brush each fillet with 2 teaspoons olive oil, and drizzle with the lemon juice. Season with salt and pepper. Roast for 15–20 minutes in the preheated oven or until the fish is just opaque inside.

While the fish is cooking, mix together the cooked lentils, bell peppers, toasted pine nuts, red onion, balsamic vinegar, basil, and remaining olive oil in a bowl. Season with salt and pepper. Serve each person a piece of cod topped with lentil salad.

Fish substitution—thick snapper fillets, cod, haddock, ling

three ways with marinades

ON HOT DAYS, OR WHEN LONG MARINATING TIMES ARE CALLED FOR, MARINATE FOODS IN THE REFRIGERATOR, BUT REMEMBER THAT FLAVORS WILL TAKE LONGER TO PENETRATE THE FLESH WHEN THE INGREDIENTS ARE COLD. AVOID BRUSHING MARINADE ONTO FOOD RIGHT AT THE END OF THE COOKING TIME; ALLOW IT TO COOK ON THE FOOD FOR ABOUT 5 MINUTES TO KILL ANY HARMFUL BACTERIA. FOR THE SAME REASON, IF YOU WISH TO SERVE LEFTOVER MARINADE AS A SAUCE, BOIL IT BEFOREHAND FOR AT LEAST 5 MINUTES.

blackened cajun marinade

Combine 2 tablespoons Cajun spice mix and 2 teaspoons sweet paprika with 2 tablespoons olive oil, 1 tablespoon lemon juice, 2 crushed garlic cloves, and 1 tablespoon finely chopped Italian parsley. Pour over 4 large skinless fish fillets (about 3/4 inch thick and weighing about 7 ounces each) such as snapper, blue-eye cod, ling, warehou, or mahimahi. Use your fingers to rub the spice mix evenly over the fillets and leave to marinate in the refrigerator for 1–1 1/2 hours. Melt 2 tablespoons unsalted butter in a large pan over high heat and cook the fillets, two at a time, for 1–2 minutes on the first side. Turn over and cook for another few minutes or until the fish is cooked and flakes easily. The surface should be well charred on each side. Serve with lemon halves—the lemons can be served lightly charred too, if desired. The marinade makes enough for 4 fillets.

fish tikka marinade

Mix together 1 cup yogurt, 2 finely chopped red Asian shallots, 1 tablespoon grated fresh ginger, 2 crushed garlic cloves, 2 tablespoons lemon juice, 1 teaspoon ground coriander, 1 tablespoon garam masala, 1 teaspoon paprika, 1 teaspoon chili powder, 2 tablespoons concentrated tomato purée, and 1 teaspoon salt in a shallow nonmetallic dish that is long and deep enough to fit your fish. To use, brush the marinade over 4 skinless fish fillets (total weight about 1 pound, 2 ounces) such as sea bream, snapper, grouper, orange roughy, or sea bass. Cover and leave to marinate in the refrigerator for at least 1 hour. The fish can be cooked in the oven, under the broiler, or on a charbroil pan or barbecue. Cook for about 5 minutes or until the fish is firm and opaque. Mix together 2 tablespoons chopped cilantro leaves, 1 peeled and diced short cucumber, and 1 cup yogurt. Serve alongside the fish, with cooked vegetables such as onion and bell pepper, and lemon wedges to squeeze over. The marinade makes enough for 4 fillets.

spicy asian marinade

Cut the bottom 4 inches from a stalk of lemongrass and remove and discard its outer layers. Finely chop the rest of the stalk. Discard the leafy part of the lemongrass. Finely grate a 2-inch piece of fresh ginger and put in a bowl with the lemongrass, 1 seeded and finely chopped red chili, 1 tablespoon fish sauce, 2 tablespoons lime juice, 2 tablespoons vegetable oil, and 2 tablespoons chopped cilantro leaves. Mix well. Arrange 1 pound, 10 ounces of fish strips or four 6-ounce fillets in a shallow dish and pour over the marinade. Leave for 1–1 1/2 hours, then remove the fish from the marinade and either stir-fry, if using strips, or broil or steam fillets. This marinade is suitable for flounder, sole, or other flatfish. The marinade makes enough for 4 fillets.

whole sole simmered in sake and soy

IN JAPAN, INGREDIENTS ARE FREQUENTLY SIMMERED IN FLAVORED COOKING LIQUID: SUCH RECIPES ARE CALLED *NIMONO*. IN THIS RECIPE, WHOLE FISH ARE GENTLY SIMMERED IN A MIXTURE OF STOCK, SAKE, SOY SAUCE, SUGAR, AND MIRIN. SERVE WITH RICE OR NOODLES.

bonito-flavored soup stock	1/2 sachet
superfine sugar	2 tablespoons
sake	1/3 cup
mirin	1/4 cup
Japanese soy sauce	1/3 cup
whole sole	2, about 10 ounces each, scaled and gutted
green beans	1 1/4 cups, cut into 1 1/4-inch pieces
broccoli	1 3/4 cups small florets

Put the soup stock in a large frying pan and add 2 cups boiling water. Stir to combine and add the sugar, sake, mirin, and soy sauce. Bring the mixture back to a boil and then reduce to a very gentle simmer.

Make a couple of diagonal slashes on the top side of each fish to ensure even cooking. Put the fish in the liquid, skin side up, and cover. Simmer for 5–6 minutes or until the fish is opaque and cooked. Turn the fish over halfway through the cooking time. You may need to cook each fish separately, depending on the size of your pan.

Meanwhile, blanch the beans and broccoli in boiling water until just tender. Drain and set aside.

A minute or so before the end of the cooking time, add the beans and broccoli to the simmering liquid. Serve each fish with a little of the cooking liquid spooned over it, accompanied by the vegetables.

Fish substitution—flounder

Simmer the fish until it is opaque and cooked through

Blanch the beans and broccoli in boiling water, then drain

kokoda .... serves 6

IN THIS REFRESHING FISH SALAD FROM FIJI, RAW FISH IS MARINATED IN LIME JUICE, WHICH REACTS WITH THE PROTEIN IN THE FLESH TO "COOK" THE FISH. ONLY THE FRESHEST OF FISH ARE SUITABLE FOR THIS RECIPE.

flounder	1 pound, skinless
lime juice	1/2 cup
vine-ripened tomatoes	2
coconut milk	1/2 cup
red chili	1 small, seeded and finely chopped
French shallots	2, thinly sliced
garlic	1 clove, crushed
red bell pepper	1 small, diced

Cut the fish into small cubes and put in a nonmetallic bowl. Add the lime juice and a generous pinch of salt, and mix with a nonmetallic spoon. Cover and leave to marinate in the refrigerator for at least 4 hours. Stir the fish every hour or so. You can leave the fish to marinate overnight if you prefer.

When the fish is ready, prepare the other ingredients. Score a cross in the base of each tomato. Put into boiling water for 20 seconds, then plunge into cold water. Drain and peel the skin away from the cross. Dice the tomatoes, discarding the cores and seeds.

Mix the tomatoes with the coconut milk, chili, shallots, garlic, and red bell pepper. Drain the fish and combine with the coconut mixture. Taste to check the seasoning, adding more salt if necessary. Eat immediately or chill until required.

Fish substitution—sole or any delicate white fish

Along with salt, smoke, and vinegar, lime juice has been used for centuries to preserve food. The acid in the juice causes the protein in seafood to "denature," that is, change chemically and physically, which stops biological activity and hence preserves the food. "Cooking" fish in this way has been used around the world, and various Pacific islands have similar recipes to the Fijian kokoda, all of which feature lime or lemon juice, coconut milk, and white-fleshed fish. Take care when marinating the fish, however, as the fish is tenderized only, not cooked, so it must be of good enough quality to be served raw. For an authentic touch, serve the salad in coconut half-shells.

three ways with curry

TYPICAL CURRY SPICES ARE TURMERIC, CILANTRO, CUMIN, CLOVES, CARDAMOM, GINGER, TAMARIND, CHILI, FENNEL, MUSTARD SEEDS, CINNAMON, AND FENUGREEK. TRADITIONALLY, SPICE MIXTURES FOR CURRIES WERE STONE-GROUND BY HAND AND WERE MADE FRESH EACH DAY. ONCE GROUND, SPICES QUICKLY LOSE THEIR FLAVOR AND AROMA, SO IT IS BEST TO BUY WHOLE SPICES AND GRIND THEM YOURSELF. ALTERNATIVELY, BUY ONE OF THE MANY GOOD-QUALITY COMMERCIAL CURRY PASTES OR POWDERS THAT ARE NOW AVAILABLE.

indian fish curry

Put 2 tablespoons olive oil in a frying pan and add 2 finely chopped onions. Gently fry over low heat for 10 minutes. Finely grate a 2-inch piece of fresh ginger and add to the pan with 2 crushed garlic cloves. Cook for 3 minutes. Increase the heat to medium, then add 2 tablespoons Madras (hot) curry paste and fry for another 2 minutes. Add 2 teaspoons ground coriander and cook for 2 minutes. Add 1⅔ cups coconut milk and 1½ tablespoons lime juice, and bring to a simmer. Add 1 pound, 10 ounces skinless fish pieces such as ling. Cover and simmer for 8 minutes. Serve over rice, sprinkled with chopped cilantro, if desired. Serves 4.

maharashtrian fish curry with coconut and chili

Mix together ¾ cup finely chopped creamed coconut, 2 crushed garlic cloves, 3 seeded and finely chopped small green chilies, ½ teaspoon each of ground turmeric, ground cloves, ground cinnamon, and ground cayenne pepper, 1 tablespoon tamarind purée, and ½ cup oil. Put 1 pound, 12 ounces skinless fish fillets such as pomfret, flounder, or sole in a shallow dish and spoon the marinade over. Turn the fish over, cover, and set aside in the refrigerator for 30 minutes. Heat 1 tablespoon oil in a large frying pan and, when hot, add the fish, reserving any remaining marinade. Cook the fillets, in batches if necessary, for 1 minute on each side. When cooked, and with all the fish in the pan, reduce the heat to low, and add the reserved marinade and ¾ cup coconut milk. Season with salt, cover, and gently cook the fish for 3–5 minutes or until cooked. Sprinkle with 2 tablespoons chopped cilantro leaves and serve immediately. Serves 4.

fish with curry sauce

Heat 2 tablespoons oil in a wok or sauté pan until hot. Add 1 pound, 5 ounces skinless fish fillets such as pomfret, sole, flounder, or blue-eye cod—shrimp are also good—to the wok or pan, adding them in batches if necessary. Cook for 2–3 minutes or until opaque. Transfer to a plate and cover with foil. Wipe out the inside of the wok or pan with paper towels and add another 2 tablespoons oil. Heat until hot, then add 2 crushed large garlic cloves and ⅓ cup red curry paste and fry for 30 seconds. Add 1¼ cups coconut milk, ⅓ cup fish sauce, 2 tablespoons sugar, and 2 teaspoons lemon juice, and heat through. Stir in 2 teaspoons shredded kaffir lime leaves and 2 tablespoons chopped cilantro leaves, and spoon the curry sauce over the fish. Garnish with a few extra cilantro leaves. Serves 4.

skate with black butter . . . . serves 4

THIS IS CONSIDERED BY MANY AS THE CLASSIC WAY IN WHICH TO PREPARE SKATE. BLACK OR BROWN BUTTER (*BEURRE NOIRE* AND *BEURRE NOISETTE*) HAS ACCOMPANIED FRENCH DISHES FOR HUNDREDS OF YEARS. IN THIS RECIPE, IT WORKS WONDERFULLY WELL WITH THE SWEET FLAVOR OF THE SKATE.

court bouillon

white wine	1 cup
onion	1, sliced
carrot	1, sliced
bay leaf	1
black peppercorns	4
skate wings	4 x 9 ounces, skinless
capers	1 tablespoon
unsalted butter	1/2 cup
Italian parsley	1 tablespoon chopped

To make the court bouillon, place the wine, onion, carrot, bay leaf, peppercorns, and 4 cups water into a large frying pan. Bring to a boil and simmer for 20 minutes. Strain the court bouillon and return the liquid to the cleaned frying pan.

Add the skate, making sure that it is completely covered with the liquid, and simmer for 5–10 minutes (depending on the thickness of the wing) or until the flesh is opaque and flakes when tested with the point of a knife. Lift out the fish, drain, cover, and keep warm until ready to serve.

Rinse, squeeze dry, and chop the capers. Heat the butter in a frying pan and cook over moderate heat for about 2 minutes or until it turns brown to make a *beurre noisette*. Do not let it get too brown or it will taste burned. Remove from the heat and stir in the parsley and capers. Season with salt and black pepper. Pour the sauce over the fish and serve immediately with steamed, cubed potatoes and lemon wedges.

Fish substitution—fillets of flatfish, such as sole or flounder, or snapper or perch

Simmer the skate until it is opaque and flakes when tested

Rinse, squeeze dry, and chop the capers

Cook the butter over moderate heat until it is golden brown

the perfect steamed fish

Steaming is a very gentle way to cook fish. If done properly, it is a wonderful way to retain the natural moistness, flavor, texture, and shape of the fish. Steaming does not have to mean boring, bland-tasting fish, as it often did in the past, but—and this is true of any fish recipe—it does depend on the freshest of fish being used. Steamed fish is particularly common in Asian cuisine.

Most fish can be successfully steamed, although oily fish, such as tuna and mackerel, are best avoided. A multitude of flavorings can be added to the fish while it is cooking, but take care not to overwhelm the natural flavor of the fish. For delicately flavored fish such as turbot and sea bass, just a sprig or two of herbs will suffice. However, for milder-tasting fish, try adding larger quantities of herbs, chilies, spices, or sauces for an extra flavor boost.

Asian bamboo steamers are ideal, but must be washed and thoroughly dried after use to remove any fishy smell. Metal steamers are also suitable. Put 2–3 inches water into a saucepan and bring to a simmer. Put a plate, or a circle of baking paper that has been pricked with a skewer, in the steamer. Pile the plate or paper with any aromatics to be used and set the fish on top, topping the fish with additional aromatics if desired. Cover with a lid and steam until the fish is just cooked through. For thin fillets, this can be as little 4–5 minutes; thicker fillets (around 1 pound) may take up to 8–10 minutes. Make sure the simmering water does not touch the fish at any point. Be careful not to overcook the fish; it should be only just cooked through. White fish turns opaque when cooked, so check if the fish is cooked by piercing with a knife to see if the middle is also opaque. Any liquid on the plate can be drizzled over the fish when serving.

barbecued gar with pesto .... serves 4

GAR ARE QUICK AND EASY TO COOK ON THE BARBECUE. THEY ARE USUALLY SOLD WHOLE AS FRESH FISH OR
BUTTERFLY FILLETS AND HAVE LOVELY SWEET AND TASTY FLESH. TAKE THE TIME TO BONE THEM CAREFULLY, AS THEY
CAN BE QUITE BONY.

gar	8, scaled, boned, and butterflied
olive oil	1 cup
rosemary	1 tablespoon chopped
thyme	1 tablespoon chopped
butternut squash	1 pound, 9 ounces, peeled
red onions	2 small

pesto
Italian parsley	1 cup
garlic	2 cloves, peeled
macadamia nuts	1/4 cup
Parmesan cheese	1 cup, grated
olive oil	2/3 cup

Pat the gar dry and place in a nonmetallic container. Season the fish on both sides with salt and pepper. Mix the oil with the rosemary and thyme, and drizzle over the fish. Leave to marinate for an hour or so or until you are ready to cook.

Meanwhile, slice the butternut squash and cut into even-sized shapes measuring approximately $2\frac{1}{2}$ x 2 x $\frac{1}{2}$ inch. Slice the onions in half widthwise.

To make the pesto, place all the ingredients in a food processor and purée to a paste. Alternatively, finely chop all the ingredients by hand and mix. Season to taste.

Preheat the barbecue or a hot plate to medium heat. Grill the vegetables and the fish for 2–3 minutes on each side, brushing regularly with the remaining herb oil. You will need a wide spatula to turn the squash on the barbecue. Serve the fish atop a few squash slices and some of the red onion. Put a generous spoonful of pesto on top.

Fish substitution—whiting, sardines, mackerel

To butterfly the gar, first scale, gut, and clean them

Remove the heads and open out the fish, pressing them flat

Lift out the bones; they should come away in one piece

shellfish

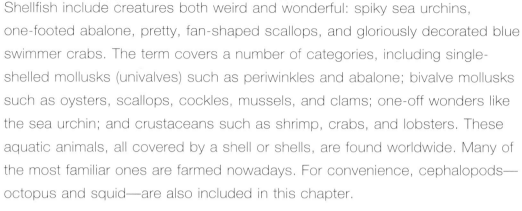

Shellfish include creatures both weird and wonderful: spiky sea urchins, one-footed abalone, pretty, fan-shaped scallops, and gloriously decorated blue swimmer crabs. The term covers a number of categories, including single-shelled mollusks (univalves) such as periwinkles and abalone; bivalve mollusks such as oysters, scallops, cockles, mussels, and clams; one-off wonders like the sea urchin; and crustaceans such as shrimp, crabs, and lobsters. These aquatic animals, all covered by a shell or shells, are found worldwide. Many of the most familiar ones are farmed nowadays. For convenience, cephalopods—octopus and squid—are also included in this chapter.

In many countries, shellfish are embraced as food rather gingerly; in others they are wholeheartedly adopted. The perception that they are difficult to prepare may have something to do with it, but whether eaten raw or marinated, stuffed, steamed, fried, boiled, baked, or barbecued, shellfish offer flavors, aromas, and textures that can be unbeatable. The recipes in this chapter have been chosen to illustrate how shellfish can be used in dishes from summer to winter, ranging from light to hearty and elaborate to surprisingly simple.

Like fish, shellfish need care when buying. Planning ahead is a necessary part of cooking with fish and shellfish, but it can also add to the pleasure. Once you have found a fishmonger you trust, you can be as adventurous as you like.

When buying shellfish, live specimens offer the best flavor, although many are available frozen. Crab and lobster are sometimes sold already cooked; the meat should smell sweet and look fresh. Cooked lobster tails should be tightly curled. Cephalopods are sold fresh and frozen, either fully intact or cleaned, and many larger fresh octopuses are also sold ready for use. If buying fresh cephalopods, use them within 1 to 2 days, or freeze fresh octopus for up to 3 months.

Live shellfish do not last long, so buy them on the day you intend to eat them and store in the refrigerator covered with a damp cloth. Always remove the dark intestinal tracts from shrimp and lobsters and the stomach sacs from lobsters and crabs before cooking. Scrub any dirty shells and remove any barnacles. Drain and rinse once or twice more in water. The general rule for cooking shellfish is to do so either very briefly or for a very long time—anything in the middle tends to result in tough meat. In these recipes, follow the preparation and cooking instructions carefully and, as with fish, if you buy good-quality shellfish from a reputable source, you have made the best of beginnings.

vietnamese rice paper rolls .... serves 4–6

ALTHOUGH THIS RECIPE MAY SOUND FIDDLY, ONCE YOU'VE GOT THE HANG OF MAKING THE ROLLS—WHICH WON'T TAKE LONG AT ALL—YOU'LL FIND THIS RECIPE TO BE EASY AND QUICK. THE RICE PAPER ROLLS ARE VERY LIGHT AND FRESH TASTING, AND MAKE A GREAT LIGHT LUNCH OR STARTER.

dried mung bean vermicelli	2½ cups
rice paper wrappers	20–25, about 6¼ inches in diameter
mint	40 leaves
cooked shrimp	20 large, cut in half horizontally
garlic chives	10, halved

dipping sauce

satay sauce	2 tablespoons
hoisin sauce	¼ cup
red chili	1, finely chopped
unsalted peanuts	1 tablespoon roasted and chopped
lemon juice	1 tablespoon

Soak the vermicelli for 5 minutes in enough hot water to cover. Drain well and use scissors to roughly chop the noodles into shorter lengths.

Using a pastry brush, brush both sides of each rice paper wrapper with water. Leave for about 2 minutes or until the wrappers become soft and pliable. Stack the wrappers on top of each other, sprinkling each lightly with water to prevent them from sticking together and drying out. Be careful, as the wrappers tear easily when softened.

Put one softened wrapper on a work surface and spoon about 1 tablespoon of the noodles along the bottom third of the wrapper, leaving enough space at the sides to fold the wrapper over. Top with two mint leaves, two shrimp halves, and half a garlic chive. Fold in the sides toward each other and firmly roll up the wrapper, allowing the garlic chive to point out of one side. Repeat with the remaining wrappers and ingredients and put the rolls on a serving plate, seam side down.

To make the dipping sauce, combine the satay sauce, hoisin sauce, red chili, peanuts, and lemon juice in a small bowl and mix thoroughly. Serve with the rolls.

Brush both sides of each rice paper wrapper with water

Put the vermicelli into a bowl and use scissors to cut them up

Roll up the rice paper wrapper to firmly enclose the filling

crab bisque..serves 4

BISQUE IS A SEASONED PURÉE OF SHELLFISH FLAVORED WITH CREAM AND BRANDY, WHICH IS USED AS THE BASIS FOR A SOUP. THE SHELLS OF THE FEATURED SEAFOOD—SUCH AS CRAB, CRAYFISH, OR LOBSTER—ARE TRADITIONALLY USED TO ADD FLAVOR, AND A SMALL AMOUNT OF THE FLESH IS RESERVED AS A GARNISH.

live crabs	2 pounds, 4 ounces
butter	1/4 cup
carrot	1/2, finely chopped
onion	1/2, finely chopped
celery	1 stalk, finely chopped
bay leaf	1
thyme	2 sprigs
concentrated tomato purée	2 tablespoons
brandy	2 tablespoons
dry white wine	2/3 cup
fish stock	4 cups
medium-grain rice	1/3 cup
heavy cream	1/4 cup
cayenne pepper	1/4 teaspoon or to taste

Freeze the crabs for 1–2 hours to immobilize them, then clean them and detach the claws.

Heat the butter in a large saucepan. Add the vegetables, bay leaf, and thyme and cook over medium heat for 3 minutes without allowing the vegetables to color. Add the crab claws, legs, and bodies and cook for 5 minutes or until the crab shells turn red. Add the concentrated tomato purée, brandy, and white wine and simmer for 2 minutes or until reduced by half.

Add the stock and 2 cups water and bring to a boil. Reduce the heat and simmer for 5 minutes. Remove the shells, leaving the crab meat in the stock, and reserve the claws to use as a garnish. Finely crush the shells in a mortar and pestle (or in a food processor with a little of the stock). Return the crushed shells to the soup with the rice. Bring to a boil, reduce the heat, cover, and simmer for about 20 minutes or until the rice is soft.

Immediately strain the bisque into a clean saucepan through a fine sieve lined with damp cheesecloth, pressing down firmly on the solids to extract all the liquid. Add the cream and season with salt and cayenne pepper, then gently reheat. Ladle into warmed soup bowls and garnish with the crab claws.

Shellfish substitution—lobster, shrimp

Remove the large body shell from the immobilized crab

Remove and discard the fibrous "dead man's fingers"

Using a sharp knife, cut the body of the crab into pieces

bouillabaisse..serves 6

FISHERMEN TRADITIONALLY MADE THIS FRENCH STEW IN LARGE CAULDRONS ON THE BEACH. IT CONTAINED THE FISH THAT WAS THE LEAST SUITABLE TO BE SOLD AT THE MARKET, SUCH AS ROCKFISH, AS WELL AS VARIOUS SHELLFISH. USE FIRM FISH SUCH AS SEA BASS, SNAPPER, OR RED MULLET; LOBSTER AND CRAB ARE GOOD, TOO.

rouille

red bell pepper	1 small
white bread	1 slice, crusts removed
red chili	1
garlic	2 cloves
egg yolk	1
olive oil	1/3 cup
oil	2 tablespoons
fennel bulb	1, thinly sliced
onion	1, chopped
vine-ripened tomatoes	1 pound, 10 ounces
concentrated tomato purée	4 tablespoons
fish stock or water	5 cups
saffron threads	a pinch
bouquet garni	1
orange zest	2-inch piece
fish fillets	3 pounds, 5 ounces, cut into bite-sized pieces
black mussels	18, cleaned
bread or toast	to serve

To make the rouille, preheat the broiler. Cut the bell pepper in half lengthwise, remove the seeds and membrane, and place skin side up under the hot broiler until the skin blackens and blisters. (Alternatively, hold the bell pepper over the gas flame of your stove until the skin is blackened.) Allow to cool before peeling away the skin. Roughly chop the bell pepper flesh. Soak the bread in 1/4 cup water, then squeeze dry with your hands. Put the bell pepper, bread, chili, garlic, and egg yolk in a mortar and pestle or food processor and pound or mix together. Gradually add the oil in a thin stream, pounding or mixing until the rouille is smooth and has the texture of thick mayonnaise. Cover and refrigerate until needed.

Heat the oil in a large saucepan and cook the fennel and onion for 5 minutes or until golden.

Meanwhile, score a cross in the base of each tomato. Cover with boiling water for 30 seconds, then plunge into cold water. Drain and peel the skin away from the cross. Chop the tomatoes, discarding the cores. Add the chopped tomato to the saucepan and cook for 3 minutes. Stir in the stock, saffron, bouquet garni, and orange zest. Bring to a boil and cook for 10 minutes.

Remove the bouquet garni and orange zest and either push the soup through a sieve or purée in a blender. Return the soup to the cleaned saucepan, season well, and bring back to a boil. Reduce the heat to a simmer and add the fish and mussels. Cook for 5 minutes or until the fish is tender and the mussels have opened. Throw away any mussels that haven't opened in this time. Serve the soup with the rouille and bread or toast.

Note: A bouquet garni is used for flavoring soups and stews. You can buy dried ones in the supermarket (look near the rest of the herbs) or make your own by wrapping the green part of a leek around a bay leaf, a sprig of thyme, a sprig of parsley, and celery leaves. Tie the bundle with kitchen string.

Roast or broil the bell pepper until the skin blisters and blackens

Using your hands, squeeze dry the soaked bread

lobster soup with zucchini and avocado ....serves 4

TO ENSURE QUALITY, IT IS BEST TO BUY A LIVE LOBSTER OR, IF NECESSARY, A DEAD COOKED ONE (NEVER BUY A DEAD UNCOOKED LOBSTER). TO HUMANELY KILL A LOBSTER, PUT IT IN THE FREEZER FOR 1–2 HOURS TO IMMOBILIZE IT, THEN PLUNGE IT INTO BOILING WATER.

butter	1/4 cup
garlic	1 clove, crushed
French shallots	2, finely chopped
onion	1, chopped
zucchini	1, diced
dry white wine	2 1/2 tablespoons
fish stock	1 2/3 cups
raw lobster meat	9 ounces, chopped
heavy cream	1 cup
avocado	1, diced
cilantro leaves	1 tablespoon chopped
parsley	1 tablespoon chopped
lemon juice	to serve

Melt the butter in a large saucepan. Add the garlic, chopped shallots, onion, and zucchini and cook over medium heat for 8–10 minutes or until the vegetables are just soft.

Add the wine and bring to a boil, boiling it for 3 minutes. Pour in the stock and bring to a boil again. Reduce the heat to low, add the chunks of lobster, and simmer for 3–4 minutes or until the lobster meat is opaque and tinged pink. Gently stir in the cream and season with salt and freshly ground black pepper.

Ladle the soup into four bowls and stir a little of the avocado, cilantro, and parsley into each one. Squeeze a little lemon juice over the soup before serving.

Shellfish substitution—crayfish, shrimp

Zucchini are baby marrows. Available in pale green, dark green, and yellow varieties, baby zucchini are perfect for fresh, raw, and lightly cooked dishes. The larger, older siblings are definitely the best for heartier, slow-cooked dishes. When shopping, look for firm, unblemished zucchini. Eat as soon as possible after purchase, as refrigeration makes their textures deteriorate. There is no need to peel them; in fact, most of the flavor is in the skin. Zucchini flowers are also edible: they are a fleeting delight of summer, available for only a few weeks each year, and are often served stuffed and fried.

rock lobster and mango salad

WHEN BUYING LIVE LOBSTERS, LOOK FOR SPECIMENS THAT ARE LIVELY AND FEEL HEAVY, AND THAT HAVE A HARD SHELL AND NO MISSING LIMBS. THE LOBSTER'S TAIL SHOULD BE TUCKED UNDER THE BODY. LARGE LOBSTERS ARE CHEAPER, BUT WEIGHT FOR WEIGHT, SMALLER SPECIMENS ARE A BETTER VALUE.

live rock lobster	1 pound, 12 ounces
sugar snap peas	1 1/3 cups, trimmed
mango	1 large, cut into small chunks
scallions	2, trimmed and sliced diagonally into small pieces
orange bell pepper	1/2, thinly sliced
short cucumber	1/2, peeled, seeded, and sliced into long, thin batons

dressing

limes	zest and juice of 2
Thai fish sauce	1 tablespoon
red chili	1 small, seeded and finely chopped
olive oil	2 tablespoons
sesame oil	1 teaspoon
dark soy sauce	1 teaspoon
sugar	1/2 teaspoon

Immobilize the rock lobster by placing it in the freezer for 1 hour. Bring a large saucepan of salted water to a boil. Drop the lobster into the water and bring back to a boil. Cook for 25 minutes, by which time the lobster will have turned red. Lift out of the pan and leave to cool. Once cool, remove the cooked meat from the shell: First, remove the head by twisting or cutting it off. Cut down the center of the underside of the tail with a pair of scissors. Peel open the tail and carefully pull out the flesh in one piece. Cut into chunks and place in a large bowl.

Bring a small saucepan of water to a boil, add the sugar snap peas, and blanch for 2 minutes. Refresh under cold running water, pat dry, and add to the lobster flesh with the mango, scallions, bell pepper, and cucumber.

Mix the dressing ingredients together in a pitcher and pour over the lobster and mango. Toss everything together and serve.

Shellfish substitution—crayfish, lobster

Remove the head of the cooked lobster by twisting

Remove the meat from the tail of the lobster in one piece

Slice the tail meat crosswise into large chunks

cuban-style shrimp with rum
.... serves 4

ALWAYS REMOVE THE BLACK THREADLIKE VEIN, OR INTESTINAL TRACT, FROM SHRIMP BEFORE COOKING THEM. WITH PRACTICE, THIS WILL COME AWAY WITH THE HEAD OF THE SHRIMP WHEN IT IS PULLED OFF. THE VEIN CAN ALSO BE REMOVED BY SLITTING OPEN THE BACK OF A PEELED SHRIMP WITH A SMALL KNIFE.

white rum	1/2 cup
hot pepper sauce	a few drops
lime	zest and juice of 1
Worcestershire sauce	2 teaspoons
all-purpose flour	2 1/2 tablespoons
ground cumin	1 teaspoon
freshly grated nutmeg	a generous pinch
raw tiger shrimp	24, peeled and deveined, tails intact
butter	1 tablespoon
olive oil	1/3 cup
garlic	4 large cloves, crushed
Italian parsley	1 tablespoon chopped
cilantro leaves	1 tablespoon chopped

In a small bowl, mix together the rum, hot pepper sauce, lime zest and juice, and Worcestershire sauce.

Mix the flour with the cumin and nutmeg, and season with salt and freshly ground black pepper. Dip the shrimp in the seasoned flour to lightly coat before cooking.

Melt half the butter with half the oil in a large sauté or frying pan and, when hot, add half the garlic and half the shrimp. Cook for 4–5 minutes or until the shrimp have turned pink and are lightly golden on the outside. Lift onto a serving plate and keep warm. Repeat with the remaining butter, oil, garlic, and shrimp.

Pour the rum mixture into the pan and allow to bubble for 30–40 seconds, stirring. Season with salt. Mix together the parsley and cilantro. Pour the sauce over the shrimp and sprinkle with the herbs before serving.

Shellfish substitution—freshwater crayfish

Shrimp are found worldwide in cold and warm waters, but the lovely big tiger shrimp (left) that are so welcome on summer barbecues are warm-water tropical creatures. In Australia, most tiger shrimp are trawled, then put in ice-cold seawater to maintain freshness on the way to the market. Elsewhere, huge farms have been established, leading to a high incidence of disease and environmental problems, in some cases. These concerns should not turn you off tiger shrimp, but rather encourage you to hunt out good-quality ones, as their taste, firm texture, and versatility are worth it. Most supplies in the Northern Hemisphere are frozen; in this case, raw is better than cooked.

three ways with shrimp

UNLIKE OTHER CRUSTACEANS, SHRIMP ARE NOT GENERALLY SOLD LIVE. THEY MAY BE SOLD RAW OR COOKED, WITH OR WITHOUT THEIR SHELLS, OR FROZEN. WHENEVER POSSIBLE, BUY THEM WITH THE SHELL ON, AS THEY WILL HAVE THE BEST FLAVOR. SHRIMP SHOULD LOOK HEALTHY AND SMELL OF THE SEA; ANY UNPLEASANT OR FISHY SMELL USUALLY MEANS THEIR FLESH HAS STARTED TO DETERIORATE. TAKE CARE TO COOK SHRIMP ONLY UNTIL THEY TURN PINK AND CURL UP; OVERCOOKING WILL MAKE THE FLESH TOUGH.

shrimp with garlic, chili, and parsley

Heat 1 tablespoon butter and ½ cup olive oil together in a large frying pan. When hot, add 2 finely chopped large garlic cloves and 1 seeded and finely chopped small red chili. Cook, stirring all the time, for 30 seconds. Add 24 large raw shrimp, peeled and deveined but with tails intact, and cook for 3–4 minutes on each side or until they turn pink. Sprinkle the shrimp with 3 tablespoons chopped Italian parsley and serve immediately on hot plates with lemon wedges. Serves 4.

drunken shrimp

Put 24 peeled and deveined large raw shrimp in a nonmetallic bowl. Mix together ⅔ cup Chinese rice wine with 2 thinly sliced red chilies, 1 teaspoon finely grated fresh ginger, and 2 teaspoons sugar and pour over the shrimp. Leave to marinate for 30 minutes. Heat a wok until very hot. Take ¼ cup of the liquid out of the marinade and add to the wok. Heat it until it is very hot, then light it either with a match or by tipping the side of the wok toward the gas flame. Let the flame burn and die down before adding the rest of the marinade and shrimp. Cook for 2–3 minutes or until the shrimp turn pink. Serve immediately. Serves 4.

Note: Chinese rice wine (also called Shaoxing rice wine) is a fermented rice wine with a rich, sweetish taste, similar to dry sherry.

tandoori shrimp pizza

Preheat the oven to 425°F. To make the tandoori sauce, heat 1 tablespoon olive oil in a frying pan over medium heat. Add 2 teaspoons ground paprika, ½ teaspoon ground cumin, ¼ teaspoon ground cardamom, ¼ teaspoon ground ginger, and ¼ teaspoon cayenne pepper. Cook until the oil starts to bubble, then cook for an additional minute. Stir in ⅓ cup yogurt, 1 teaspoon lemon juice, and 2 crushed garlic cloves. Then add 16 large raw shrimp, peeled and deveined, with tails intact. Cook for 5 minutes or until the shrimp turn pink. Remove the shrimp from the tandoori sauce with a slotted spoon and spread the sauce over a 12-inch ready-made pizza base, leaving a ½-inch border. Slice 1 onion and 1 small red bell pepper and sprinkle half of each over the pizza base. Arrange the shrimp on top. Top with the remaining onion and bell pepper and bake for about 20 minutes. Sprinkle with 3 tablespoons torn basil, then serve with dollops of extra yogurt. Serves 4.

warm shrimp, arugula, and feta salad

serves 6

ARUGULA AND SHRIMP SEEM TO HAVE A PARTICULAR AFFINITY, WITH THE PEPPERY BITE OF THE LEAVES COMPLEMENTING THE SWEET, FIRM FLESH OF THE SHRIMP. THIS SALAD IS PERFECT FOR THE HEIGHT OF SUMMER, WHEN RIPE, JUICY TOMATOES ARE AT THEIR BEST AND MOST ABUNDANT.

scallions	4, chopped
plum tomatoes	4, chopped
red bell pepper	1, chopped
canned chickpeas	2$\frac{1}{2}$ cups, rinsed and drained
dill	1 tablespoon chopped
basil	3 tablespoons finely shredded
extra-virgin olive oil	$\frac{1}{4}$ cup
butter	$\frac{1}{4}$ cup
raw shrimp	2 pounds, 4 ounces, peeled and deveined, tails intact
red chilies	2 small, finely chopped
garlic	4 cloves, crushed
lemon juice	2 tablespoons
wild or baby arugula	2 bunches
feta cheese	1$\frac{1}{3}$ cups

Put the scallions, tomatoes, bell pepper, chickpeas, dill, and shredded basil in a large bowl and toss together well.

Heat the oil and butter in a large frying pan or wok, add the shrimp, and cook, stirring, over high heat for 3 minutes. Add the chili and garlic and continue cooking for another 2 minutes or until the shrimp turn pink. Remove the pan from the heat and stir in the lemon juice.

Gently toss the arugula leaves with the tomato and chickpea mixture. Arrange on a large serving platter and top with the shrimp mixture. Crumble the feta cheese over the top and serve.

The chickpea is a small legume whose lineage goes back to ancient Egypt and the Levant. It is still popular in those areas, as well as in parts of the Mediterranean, the Middle East, and India. Dried chickpeas require long soaking and cooking times to render them soft; canned chickpeas need only thorough rinsing before use. Chickpeas have a meaty sweetness to them, and famous uses include dishes such as hummus, falafel, and Indian dhal. In combination with seafood, shrimp seem to be the standout choice—the filling nature of chickpeas nicely balances the lighter flavor of shrimp and other summer salad ingredients.

sugarcane shrimp with dipping sauce . . . . makes 8

IT MAY BE DIFFICULT TO FIND FRESH PIECES OF SUGARCANE. CANS OF PEELED, READY-TO-USE CANE PIECES ARE AVAILABLE FROM SOME ASIAN SUPERMARKETS. OR LOOK FOR PACKAGED PIECES, WHICH HAVE BEEN BOILED TO MAKE THEM EDIBLE; PEEL AWAY THE BROWNISH SKIN FROM THE WHITE FLESH BEFORE USING.

raw shrimp	14 ounces, peeled and deveined
egg white	1
ground coriander	1 teaspoon
red Asian shallots	2, peeled and roughly chopped
garlic	3 cloves, peeled and roughly chopped
palm sugar	1 teaspoon grated (soft brown sugar can be substituted)
fish sauce	1 teaspoon
lemongrass	1 stem, white part only, cut into three pieces
Vietnamese mint or other mint leaves	1 tablespoon chopped
salt	1 teaspoon
sugarcane	8 x thin 4-inch lengths, about 1/2 inch in diameter, peeled (if the pieces are thick, cut them lengthwise into quarters)
oil	for deep-frying

dipping sauce

rice vinegar	1 tablespoon
lime juice	1 tablespoon
fish sauce	1 tablespoon
sambal oelek	1/4 teaspoon (see note)
sugar	1 teaspoon
cucumber	1 tablespoon, peeled and finely diced

Put the shrimp in a food processor with half the egg white and the ground coriander, shallots, garlic, palm sugar, fish sauce, lemongrass, mint, and salt. Process to a paste. Alternatively, chop finely and mix by hand. Add just enough of the remaining egg white to bind the mixture. Tip the mixture out onto a large plate. Cover and chill for 30 minutes in the refrigerator.

Combine all the ingredients for the dipping sauce in a small bowl.

Divide the shrimp mixture into eight equal portions. Put a portion of the shrimp mixture in the palm of your hand. Press the end of a piece of sugarcane into the middle of the mixture, then firmly mold the mixture around the cane in a sausage shape so that it covers about 2 1/2 inches of the cane. Transfer to a board and repeat with the remaining shrimp and pieces of cane to make eight sugarcane shrimps in total.

Fill a deep-fat fryer or large saucepan one-third full of oil. Heat the oil to 350°F or until a cube of white bread dropped into the oil browns in 15 seconds.

Cook three shrimp sticks at a time for 4–5 minutes or until the shrimp mixture turns a light golden brown. Turn halfway through cooking to ensure they brown evenly. Remove and drain on crumpled paper towels. Cool for a few minutes before serving with the dipping sauce.

Note: Sambal oelek is a hot paste made from fresh red chilies and other seasonings. It is sold in jars in the Asian section of the supermarket and will keep for months if stored in the refrigerator.

three ways with mayonnaise

MAYONNAISE IS SIMPLY AN EMULSION OF EGG YOLKS, SALT, OIL, AN ACID SUCH AS VINEGAR, AND SOMETIMES MUSTARD OR OTHER FLAVORINGS. MAKING YOUR OWN MAYONNAISE IS WELL WORTH THE EFFORT. HAVE YOUR INGREDIENTS AT ROOM TEMPERATURE, AND WHEN YOU START TO MIX, ALWAYS ADD THE OIL DROP BY DROP. ONCE THE MAYONNAISE HAS BEGUN TO EMULSIFY, CONTINUE ADDING THE OIL IN A SLOW STREAM. IF IT CURDLES, SIMPLY ADD THE MIXTURE, A LITTLE AT A TIME, TO ANOTHER EGG YOLK, BEATING WELL AFTER EACH ADDITION.

lime mayonnaise

Put 2 large egg yolks in a bowl along with a little salt and freshly ground black pepper, and gently mix together with a whisk. Mix 1/2 cup each of peanut and olive oil together in a pitcher. Slowly add the oil to the egg yolks, drop by drop, whisking all the time. Increase to a slow trickle as the mayonnaise begins to thicken. Fold in the zest of 1 lime, the juice of half the lime, and 1 tablespoon chopped dill. Taste the mayonnaise and season to your liking with a little extra lime juice, salt, and freshly ground black pepper if needed. Serve with cold cooked seafood such as lobster, shrimp, and white fish. Serves 4.

herb aioli

Put 4 egg yolks, 4 crushed garlic cloves, 1 tablespoon chopped basil, 4 tablespoons chopped Italian parsley, and 1 tablespoon lemon juice in a mortar or food processor. Pound with the pestle or process until light and creamy. Add 3/4 cup olive oil, drop by drop, from the tip of a teaspoon, pounding or processing constantly until the mixture begins to thicken. At this point, add the oil in a steady stream until all the oil is incorporated and the mayonnaise is thick. (If you are using a food processor, pour in the oil in a thin stream with the motor running.) This sauce goes well with a range of cooked seafood such as lobster, mussels, scallops, shrimp, and salmon. Serves 4.

vodka and chili mayonnaise

Seed and finely chop 1–2 small red chilies and put in a mortar or food processor with 4 egg yolks. Pound with the pestle or process until light and creamy and the chili is well mixed into the eggs. Add 2/3 cup olive oil, drop by drop, from the tip of a teaspoon, pounding or processing constantly until the mixture begins to thicken. At this point, add the oil in a steady stream until all the oil is incorporated and the mayonnaise is thick. (If you are using a food processor, pour in the oil in a thin stream with the motor running.) Add 2 teaspoons vodka, season with salt and freshly ground black pepper, and mix well. This sauce goes well with smoked salmon or trout, or most types of cold cooked seafood. Makes 3/4 cup. Serves 4.

shrimp with lime mayonnaise

mexican seafood stew with avocado salsa..serves 4

AFTER BEING INTRODUCED TO MEXICO BY THE INVADING SPANIARDS MORE THAN 400 YEARS AGO, CILANTRO WAS QUICKLY EMBRACED IN LOCAL DISHES, AS ITS STRONG, FRESH FLAVOR COMPLEMENTS THE SPICINESS OF THEIR EVER-POPULAR CHILI. SERVE THIS DISH WITH SOURDOUGH OR OTHER RUSTIC BREAD.

olive oil	¼ cup
onion	1 large, chopped
celery	1 large stalk, chopped
garlic	3 cloves, crushed
thin red chilies	2 small, seeded and finely chopped
fish stock	¾ cup
canned plum tomatoes	1 pound, 12 ounces
bay leaves	2
dried oregano	1 teaspoon
superfine sugar	1 teaspoon
corn	2 large cobs, kernels removed
halibut fillets	1 pound, 2 ounces, skinless
cilantro leaves	2 tablespoons, chopped
limes	juice of 2
raw jumbo shrimp	12, peeled and deveined, tails intact
scallops	8
clams	12, cleaned
heavy cream	½ cup

avocado salsa

avocado	½ small
red onion	½ small, finely chopped
cilantro leaves	1 tablespoon chopped
lime	finely grated zest and juice of 1

Heat the oil in a large saucepan. Add the onion and celery and cook over medium–low heat for 10 minutes, stirring occasionally. Add the garlic and chilies and cook for 1 minute, stirring. Add the fish stock and tomatoes and break the tomatoes up in the pan using a wooden spoon.

Stir in the bay leaves, oregano, and sugar and bring to a boil. Allow to bubble for 2 minutes, then reduce the heat to low and gently simmer for 10 minutes. Allow to cool for 5 minutes, then remove the bay leaves and tip the mixture into a food processor or blender and blend until fairly smooth, but still retaining some texture. Alternatively, push the mixture through a coarse sieve by hand.

Return the mixture to the pan and season with salt. Add the corn kernels and bring back to a boil. Reduce the heat to a simmer to cook for 3 minutes or until the kernels are just tender. Cut the fish into large chunks.

Stir the cilantro and lime juice into the mixture, add the fish, then simmer gently for 1 minute. Add the shrimp and scallops and sprinkle the clams on top. Cover with a lid and cook gently for an additional 2–3 minutes or until the seafood is opaque and cooked through and the clams have steamed open. Discard any clams that do not open during cooking.

While the fish is poaching, make the avocado salsa. Chop the avocado into small cubes and mix with the red onion, cilantro, and lime zest and juice. Season with salt and freshly ground black pepper. Before serving, stir the cream into the stew, ladle into deep bowls, and serve with the salsa.

Fish substitution—kingfish, snapper

Using a sieve or mouli, purée the tomato mixture

Add the seafood to the pan and steam until the clams open

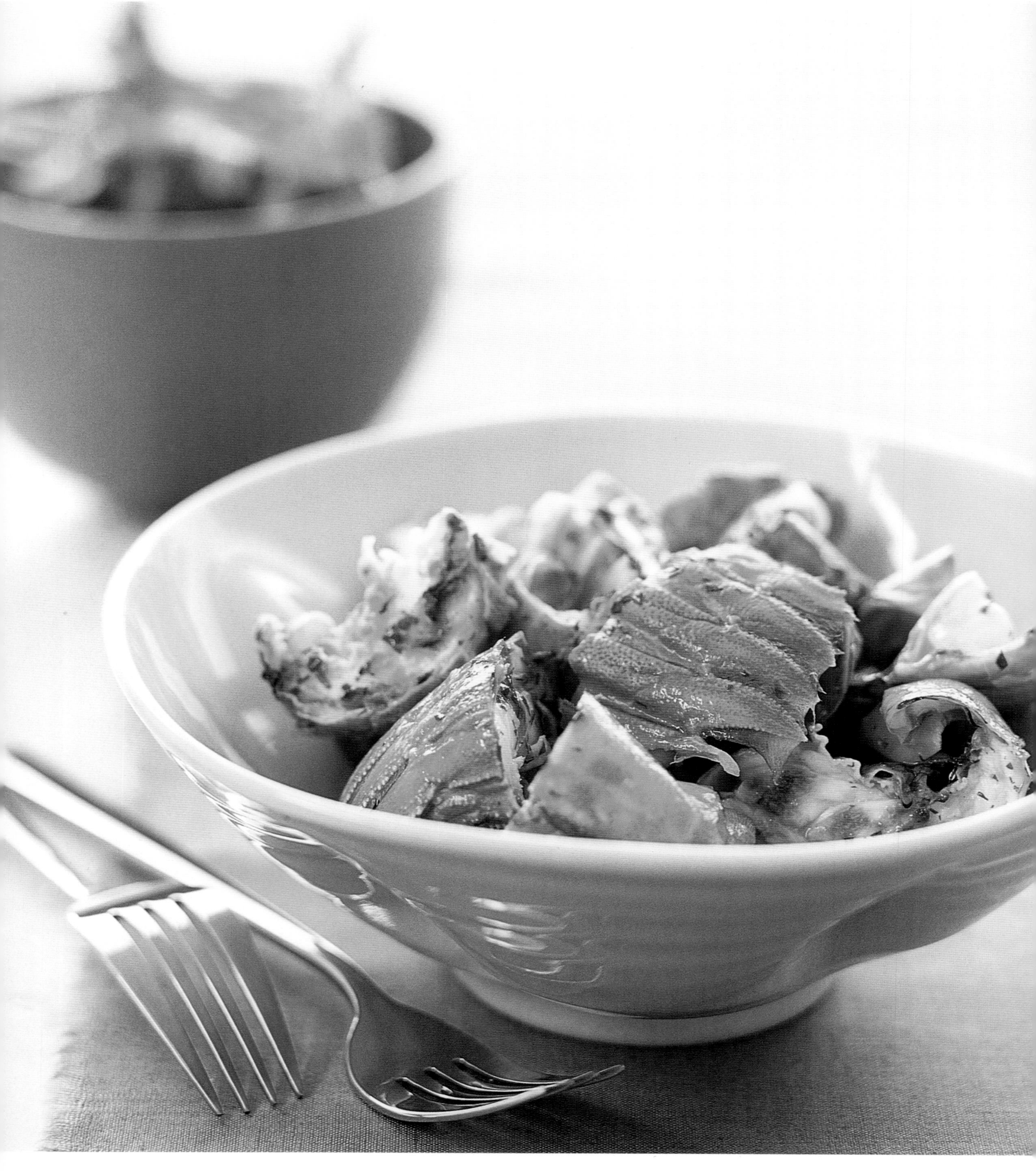

herbed bugs with sweet cider sauce

THE CURIOUSLY NAMED BUGS ARE FLATTENED CRUSTACEANS THAT HAVE A SOMEWHAT PREHISTORIC APPEARANCE AND A FLESH SIMILAR TO THAT OF CRAYFISH. THEY NEED ONLY BRIEF COOKING.

bugs	16
olive oil	1/3 cup
lemon juice	2/3 cup
garlic	3 cloves, crushed
Italian parsley	a large handful, finely chopped
dill	3 tablespoons finely chopped, plus extra to garnish
apple cider	1/3 cup
butter	2 tablespoons
crusty bread and green salad	to serve

Remove the heads from the bugs, then cut them in half lengthwise. Put them in a single layer in a shallow nonmetallic dish. Combine the olive oil, lemon juice, garlic, parsley, and dill and pour over the bugs. Cover and refrigerate for at least 1 hour.

Preheat a charbroil pan or barbecue to high. Cook the bugs, shell side down, for 2 minutes. Turn and cook for another 2 minutes or until tender. Transfer to a serving platter.

Simmer the apple cider in a small saucepan until reduced by two-thirds. Reduce the heat and add the butter, stirring until melted. Remove from the heat, pour over the bugs, and serve with crusty bread and a green salad.

Shellfish substitution—scampi, crayfish

Bugs (also known as flathead, slipper, or shovel-nosed lobsters, or Balmain or Moreton Bay bugs) belong to the family *Scyllaridae*, and are found all over the world. Their name translates to "sea cricket" in French, Italian, and Spanish, due to the cricketlike snapping noise that fishermen report hearing them make in the water. All species have the same general shape and characteristics, but vary in size and color from the 18-inch Mediterranean types to the 10-inch Indo-Pacific species. They are less well known than true lobsters, but their meat—which is contained in the tail section—can be prepared in a similar way.

three ways with crab

crab cakes with avocado salsa

Put 12 ounces fresh crab meat in a bowl. Pick out any stray pieces of shell or cartilage. Add 2 lightly beaten eggs, 1 finely chopped scallion, 1 tablespoon mayonnaise, 2 teaspoons sweet chili sauce, and $1^1/4$ cups fresh white bread crumbs. Season with salt and freshly ground black pepper, then stir well. Using wet hands, form the crab mixture into eight flat patties. Cover and refrigerate for 30 minutes. Meanwhile, make the avocado salsa. Put 2 chopped vine-ripened plum tomatoes, 1 finely chopped small red onion, 1 diced large ripe avocado, $1/4$ cup lime juice, 2 tablespoons chervil leaves, and $1/2$ teaspoon superfine sugar in a bowl. Season to taste with salt and freshly ground black pepper, then toss gently. Heat $1/4$ cup oil in a large frying pan over medium heat. Dust the patties with all-purpose flour and shallow-fry them for 3 minutes on each side or until golden brown—only turn them once so they don't break up. Drain on crumpled paper towels. Serve the crab cakes with the avocado salsa (or use the tomato salsa on page 127) and lime wedges, if desired. Serves 4.

Shellfish substitution—canned or thawed frozen crab meat

char kway teow with crab

Put 4 cups dried thin rice noodles in a bowl and cover with boiling water. Leave to soak for 10 minutes, then drain. Heat $1/4$ cup oil in a wok and when hot, add 2 thinly sliced shallots, 1 finely chopped garlic clove, and 2 finely chopped small chilies. Cook for 5 minutes, stirring. Add $2^1/2$ cups bean sprouts and 6 ounces finely chopped Chinese barbecued pork, and cook for 2 minutes. Add $1/4$ cup light soy sauce, 2 tablespoons oyster sauce, the noodles, 1 pound, 2 ounces fresh crab meat, and 2 tablespoons chopped cilantro leaves. Stir for 2 minutes to heat through. Season with salt and serve immediately. Serves 4. Note: You will need 6 live crabs, each weighing about 9 ounces, to get this amount of crab meat.

Shellfish substitution—canned or thawed frozen crab meat

spaghetti with crab and avocado

Cook 12 ounces spaghetti according to the package instructions. Drain and set aside. Meanwhile, put 7 ounces fresh crab meat in a bowl and pull out any stray pieces of shell or cartilage. Separate the meat into individual pieces. Peel a large avocado and cut into small cubes. Add to the crab along with a handful of Italian parsley leaves. In a small bowl, combine $1/2$ cup olive oil and 2 tablespoons lemon juice and season well with salt and freshly ground black pepper. Pour over the crab mixture and gently toss to mix. Add the pasta and toss again gently. Serve immediately on warm plates. Serves 4 as a starter.

Shellfish substitution—canned or thawed frozen crab meat

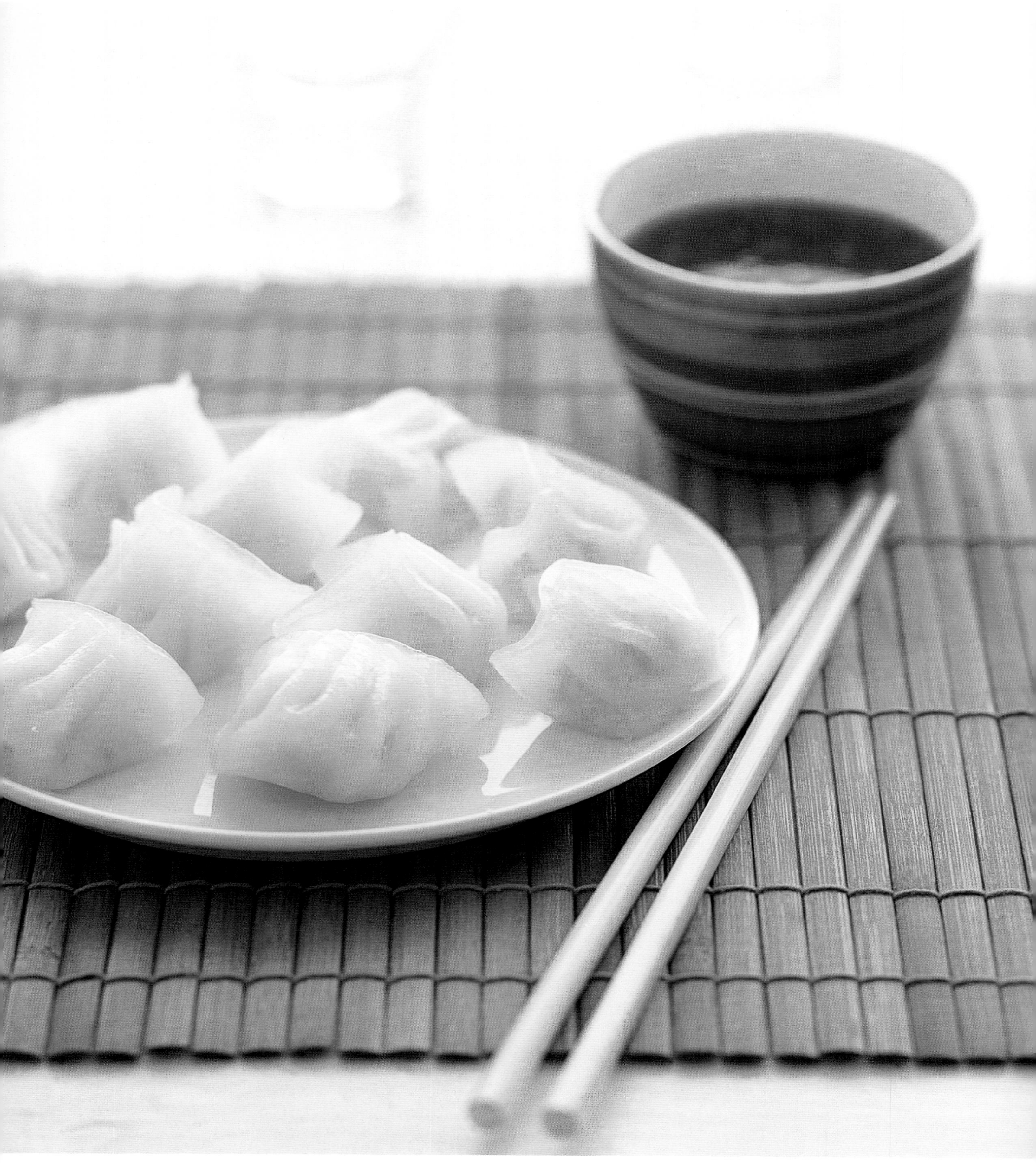

har gow .... makes 24

HAR GOW ARE ONE OF THE MANY DIM SUM SO ENJOYED BY THE CHINESE AT BREAKFAST OR LUNCH. THESE SNACKLIKE MORSELS COME IN STEAMED, FRIED, AND DEEP-FRIED VARIETIES, AND HAVE BEEN PART OF CANTONESE CUISINE SINCE THE SUNG DYNASTY NEARLY 1,000 YEARS AGO.

filling

shrimp	1 pound, 2 ounces, peeled and deveined
pork or bacon fat	1 3/4 ounces, rind removed and finely diced
bamboo shoots	1/3 cup, finely chopped
scallion	1, finely chopped
sugar	1 teaspoon
soy sauce	1 tablespoon
roasted sesame oil	1/2 teaspoon
egg white	1, lightly beaten
salt	1 teaspoon
cornstarch	1 tablespoon

dough

wheat starch	1 1/2 cups, or as needed (see note)
cornstarch	1 tablespoon
oil	2 teaspoons
soy sauce or hot chili sauce	to serve

To make the filling, cut half of the shrimp into 1/2-inch chunks. Chop the remaining shrimp using a knife or food processor until finely ground. Combine all the shrimp in a large bowl. Add the pork or bacon fat, bamboo shoots, scallion, sugar, soy sauce, sesame oil, egg white, salt, and cornstarch. Mix well to combine.

To make the dough, put the wheat starch, cornstarch, and oil in a small bowl. Add 1 cup boiling water and mix until well combined. Add a little extra starch if the dough is too sticky.

Roll the dough into a long cylinder and divide it into 24 pieces. Cover the pieces with a damp dish towel. Using a rolling pin and working with one portion of dough at a time, roll out a 3 1/2- to 4-inch round (you may find this easier if you put the dough between two pieces of oiled plastic wrap).

Put 1 teaspoon of the filling in the center of each wrapper and fold the wrapper over to make a half-moon shape. Spread a little water along the edge of the wrapper and use your thumb and index finger to form small pleats along the outside edge. With the other hand, press the two opposite edges together to seal. The inside edge should curve in a semicircle to conform to the shape of the pleated edge. Put the har gow in two bamboo steamers lined with waxed paper punched with holes. Cover the har gow as you work to prevent them from drying out. Or, if you do not have two bamboo steamers, cook the har gow in two batches.

Cover and steam the har gow over simmering water in a wok for 6–8 minutes or until the wrappers are translucent, swapping the steamers halfway through. Serve with soy or hot chili sauce.

Note: Wheat starch is a type of gluten-free flour that is used as a thickener and in dumpling wrappers. It is available in Asian stores.

Roll out portions of dough, one at a time, into rounds

Fold the dough over the filling, then pleat the edges

cajun deviled crab .... serves 4

THE TERM *DEVILED* DENOTES A DISH THAT IS COATED OR TOPPED WITH BREAD CRUMBS AND SERVED WITH A SPICY SAUCE. IF USING FRESH CRABS FOR THIS RECIPE, RESERVE THE SHELLS AND SERVE THE DEVILED CRAB IN THEM; THE MIXTURE MAKES ENOUGH TO FILL 4 SMALL TO MEDIUM SHELLS.

butter	1 tablespoon
all-purpose flour	1 1/2 tablespoons
milk	1 cup
heavy cream	1/4 cup
dijon mustard	1 tablespoon
Worcestershire sauce	1 teaspoon
cayenne pepper	a pinch
paprika	a pinch
lemon juice	2 teaspoons
Italian parsley	2 tablespoons finely chopped
cooked crab meat	3 1/2 ounces
hot pepper sauce	1 or 2 drops
white bread	1 slice, stale
Parmesan cheese	1/3 cup, grated

Melt the butter in a saucepan. Add the flour and combine to make a roux. Remove the pan from the heat and gradually add the milk, stirring after each addition. Return to the heat and gently bring to a boil, stirring constantly until thick.

Take the saucepan off the heat again and stir in the cream, mustard, Worcestershire sauce, cayenne pepper, paprika, lemon juice, half the parsley, and the crab meat. Add the hot pepper sauce and season with salt.

Preheat the oven to 400°F. Put the bread in a food processor and process to fine crumbs or grate it on a coarse grater. Mix with the cheese and the remaining parsley.

Spoon the crab mixture into the empty crab shells or use dishes with a 2/3-cup capacity. Sprinkle the bread crumb mixture over the top. Put on a baking sheet and heat in the oven for 10 minutes or until the mixture is bubbling and the bread crumbs are golden brown.

It is best to buy crabs that are alive—choose lively ones that feel heavy for their size. Never buy dead uncooked crabs. If buying cooked crabs, they should smell fresh and be undamaged, with their limbs drawn into the body. To humanely kill a crab, put it in the freezer for at least 45 minutes, then drop it into a saucepan of boiling, salted water. Simmer for 15 minutes per 1 pound. To remove the meat from a cooked crab, snap off the flap on the underside, then turn over and pull the top shell away from the bottom shell. Remove the feathery gills and stomach sac and snap off the mouth. Pick the meat out of the shells, keeping dark and white meat separate. Twist off and crack the legs and claws and take out any meat.

three ways with barbecue

TO PREPARE AND CLEAN CALAMARI OR OCTOPUS, CUT OR GENTLY PULL THE TENTACLES AWAY FROM THE TUBE; THE INTESTINES SHOULD COME AWAY WITH THEM. CUT UNDER THE EYES TO REMOVE THE INTESTINES FROM THE TENTACLES, THEN REMOVE THE BEAK (IF IT REMAINS IN THE CENTER OF THE TENTACLES) BY USING YOUR FINGERS TO PUSH UP THE CENTER. PULL AWAY THE SOFT BONE. RUB THE TUBES UNDER COLD RUNNING WATER AND THE SKIN SHOULD COME AWAY EASILY. WASH THE TUBES AND TENTACLES AND DRAIN WELL.

barbecued calamari with garlic and parsley dressing

First, prepare and clean 1 pound, 10 ounces small calamari, or ask your fishmonger to do it for you. Put the tubes and tentacles in a bowl, add $1/4$ teaspoon salt, and mix well. Cover and refrigerate for about 30 minutes. Heat the barbecue or a flatplate. Meanwhile, make the dressing. Whisk together $1/4$ cup extra-virgin olive oil, 3 tablespoons finely chopped Italian parsley, 2 crushed garlic cloves, $1/2$ teaspoon freshly ground black pepper, and some salt in a small pitcher or bowl. When ready to cook the calamari, lightly oil the barbecue or flatplate and cook the calamari in small batches for 2–3 minutes or until the tubes are white and tender. Grill the tentacles for 1 minute or until they curl up and are brown all over. Serve hot, drizzled with the dressing, and accompanied by arugula leaves and crusty bread. Serves 4.

Shellfish substitution—octopus, shrimp, or chunks of firm white fish fillet

barbecued asian-style seafood

Peel and devein 1 pound, 2 ounces raw shrimp, leaving the tails intact. Prepare and clean 1 pound, 2 ounces baby calamari and cut the tubes into quarters. Clean 1 pound, 2 ounces baby octopus. (You can also ask your fishmonger to clean both for you.) Put the seafood into a shallow nonmetallic bowl along with $10 1/2$ ounces scallop meat. In a separate bowl, combine 1 cup sweet chili sauce, 1 tablespoon fish sauce, 2 tablespoons lime juice, and 1 tablespoon peanut oil. Pour the mixture over the seafood and mix gently to coat. Allow to marinate in the refrigerator for 1 hour. Drain the seafood and reserve the marinade. Heat 2 tablespoons peanut oil on the barbecue, flatplate, or charbroil pan. Cook the seafood, in batches if necessary, over high heat for 3–5 minutes or until tender. Drizzle each batch with a little of the leftover marinade during cooking. Serve with steamed rice with lime wedges. Serves 6.

honey and lime shrimp kabobs with tomato salsa

Peel and devein 32 raw shrimp, leaving the tails intact. Put them in a nonmetallic dish. Whisk together $1/4$ cup honey, 1 seeded and finely chopped small red chili, 2 tablespoons olive oil, the zest and juice of 2 limes, 1 crushed large garlic clove, a $3/4$-inch piece of fresh, finely grated ginger, and 1 tablespoon chopped cilantro leaves. Pour the marinade over the shrimp, toss well, cover, and refrigerate for at least 3 hours, turning occasionally. Soak eight bamboo skewers in water for 30 minutes. Meanwhile, make the salsa. Score a cross in the base of 2 tomatoes. Cover with boiling water for 30 seconds, then plunge into cold water. Peel the skin away from the cross. Dice the tomatoes, discarding the cores and saving any juice. In a bowl, mix the tomato flesh and juice with 1 diced just-ripe small mango, $1/2$ diced small red onion, 1 seeded and finely chopped small red chili, the zest and juice of 1 lime, and 2 tablespoons chopped cilantro leaves. Preheat the broiler or a flatplate to high. Thread 4 shrimp onto each skewer. Cook for 4 minutes, turning halfway through cooking and basting regularly with leftover marinade, until the shrimp turn pink and are lightly browned on both sides. Serve the kabobs with salsa and steamed rice. Serves 4.

zarzuela .... serves 4–6

THIS CATALAN FISH SOUP IS NAMED AFTER A STYLE OF LIGHT OPERA, WHICH GIVES SOME IDEA OF ITS VITALITY. IT INCORPORATES A VARIETY OF SEAFOOD, AND IS BUILT AROUND A PICADA. THIS BLEND OF GARLIC, NUTS, AND BREAD ACTS LIKE A ROUX TO GIVE FORM TO OR HOLD TOGETHER DISHES.

sofrito base

tomatoes	2 large, peeled
olive oil	1 tablespoon
onions	2, finely chopped
concentrated tomato purée	1 tablespoon

picada

white bread	3 slices, crusts removed
almonds	1 tablespoon, roasted
garlic	3 cloves
olive oil	1 tablespoon

lobster tail	1 raw, about 14 ounces
firm white fish fillets such as cod, warehou, or flake	1 pound, 10 ounces, skinless
all-purpose flour	**for coating, seasoned** with salt and freshly ground black pepper
olive oil	2–3 tablespoons
calamari tubes	4 1/2 ounces, cleaned and cut into rings
raw large shrimp	12
dry white wine	1/2 cup
black mussels	12–15, cleaned
brandy	1/2 cup
Italian parsley	3 tablespoons chopped

Score a cross in the base of the tomatoes. Place in a heatproof bowl and cover with boiling water. Leave for 30 seconds, then transfer to cold water and peel the skin away from the cross. To seed, cut each tomato in half and scoop out the seeds with a teaspoon. Chop the tomato flesh.

To make the sofrito base, heat the oil in a large flameproof casserole dish on the stovetop. Add the onion and stir for 5 minutes without browning. Add the chopped tomato, tomato purée, and 1/2 cup water and stir for 10 minutes. Stir in another 1/2 cup water, season, and set the dish aside.

To make the picada, finely chop the bread, almonds, and garlic in a food processor or by hand. With the motor running, or continuously stirring, gradually add the oil to form a paste.

Preheat the oven to 350°F. Cut the lobster tail into rounds through the membrane that separates the shell segments and set aside. Cut the fish fillets into bite-sized pieces and lightly coat in flour. Heat the oil in a large frying pan and fry the fish in batches over medium heat for 2–3 minutes or until cooked and golden brown all over. Add to the casserole dish with the sofrito.

Add a little oil to the frying pan if necessary, add the calamari, and cook, stirring, for 1–2 minutes. Remove and add to the fish. Cook the lobster and shrimp for 2–3 minutes or until just pink, then add to the casserole. Add the wine to the pan and bring to a boil. Reduce the heat, add the mussels, cover, and steam for 4–5 minutes. Add to the casserole, discarding any unopened mussels.

Pour the brandy into the same pan and ignite. When the flames have died down, pour over the seafood. Mix well, cover, and bake for 20 minutes. Stir in the picada and cook for 10 minutes more or until warmed through—do not overcook or the seafood will toughen. Sprinkle with the parsley.

Note: Raw lobster tails are available frozen.

crayfish with
dill and melted butter .... serves 2

CRAYFISH ARE SMALL FRESHWATER CRUSTACEANS, SIMILAR IN APPEARANCE AND HABIT TO LOBSTER. THEY ARE ALSO KNOWN AS CRAWFISH IN SOME PARTS OF THE UNITED STATES, AND AS YABBIES AND MARRONS IN AUSTRALIA. CHOOSE CRAYFISH THAT FEEL HEAVY FOR THEIR SIZE.

live freshwater crayfish	1 pound
salt	1 tablespoon
sugar	2 tablespoons
dill	4 large sprigs
lemons	2
butter	1/3 cup

Immobilize the crayfish by putting them in the freezer 1 hour before you plan to cook them.

Bring a large saucepan of water to a boil with the salt, sugar, 2 dill sprigs, and 1 lemon cut in half. Reduce the heat to medium, add the crayfish, and simmer for 4–6 minutes, depending on their size. The crayfish will float when they are cooked.

Meanwhile, melt the butter and season with salt and freshly ground black pepper. Chop the remaining two sprigs of dill and stir into the butter.

Drain the crayfish well; to drain the claws thoroughly, make a small hole in each one to let any water out. Cut the crayfish in half. Hold the tail firmly in one hand with a dish towel, plunge a large, sharp kitchen knife into the midpoint, where the tail meets the head, and slice quickly down. Next, slice lengthwise through the tail. Discard the head.

Serve the crayfish tail and claws in a large bowl alongside the melted butter for dipping, with the second lemon, cut into wedges. Provide finger bowls and napkins for cleaning up.

Shellfish substitution—small lobster, langoustine, marrons, yabbies

Plunge the immobilized crayfish into the boiling cooking liquid

Cut the cooked crayfish in half where the head and tail meet

Slice the tail section in half lengthwise

the perfect tempura

Tempura is one of Japan's most widely recognized dishes. It is actually of Portuguese origin, and consists of bite-sized pieces of seafood or vegetables that are coated in a light batter and then deep-fried until crisp and puffed. The batter is usually nothing more than flour and water, although egg is sometimes added. The consistency and temperature of the batter are the all-important factors in achieving beautifully crisp tempura. Both the batter and food must be kept cold until just before cooking, and the cooking oil must be kept at a steady 350°F throughout the cooking process (using a special thermometer) to achieve light, crisp batter. Tempura is usually served with a soy sauce–based dipping sauce. Tempura flour is an especially fine flour available from Japanese food stores and large supermarkets.

Prepare the seafood to be cooked by cutting each piece into bite-sized chunks. To serve 4 as an appetizer, or as a main meal when served with rice, use 7 ounces skinless fish fillets and 12 large shrimp. Skinless haddock fillets, bream, cod, and rock cod are all good choices, as are calamari, lobster, and crayfish. Peel and devein the shrimp, leaving the tails intact, and make three cuts on the underside of each shrimp to straighten them out. Keep the seafood in the refrigerator until ready to use it. To make enough batter for 4 servings, put 1 1/4 cups tempura flour in a bowl and use chopsticks to incorporate 2/3 cup ice-cold water. Mix until just combined but still lumpy— it is important not to beat the lumps out. Add a few ice cubes to keep it cold.

Fill a deep fryer or large saucepan one-third full of vegetable oil and heat to 350°F or until a cube of white bread dropped into the oil browns in 15 seconds. Dip the fish chunks and shrimp in the batter, allowing excess batter to drip off. Fry until crisp and golden. Drain on crumpled paper towels and serve immediately with a dipping sauce. Do not let the tempura sit around and do not reheat it, as it will become soggy.

To make your own dipping sauce, stir 1 teaspoon finely grated fresh ginger and 1/2 tablespoon mirin into 1/4 cup soy sauce. Dilute it to taste with up to 1 1/2 tablespoons water. Pour the sauce into dipping bowls. This makes enough to serve 4.

shrimp pot pies .... serves 4

RAW SHRIMP SHOULD SMELL PLEASANTLY OF THE SEA. REJECT ANY THAT SMELL OFF OR FISHY, OR THAT HAVE BLACK HEADS OR ARE OOZING BLACK JUICES. FRESH RAW SHRIMP ARE THE BEST CHOICE, BUT FROZEN RAW SHRIMP MAY BE USED. THAW THEM ON A PLATE IN THE REFRIGERATOR, AND COOK WITHOUT DELAY.

butter	3 tablespoons
leek	1, white part only, thinly sliced
garlic	1 clove, finely chopped
raw shrimp	2 pounds, 4 ounces, peeled and deveined, tails intact
all-purpose flour	1 tablespoon
chicken or fish stock	3/4 cup
dry white wine	1/2 cup
cream	2 cups
lemon juice	2 tablespoons
dill	1 tablespoon chopped
Italian parsley	1 tablespoon chopped
dijon mustard	1 teaspoon
frozen puff pastry	1 sheet, just thawed
egg	1, lightly beaten
salad and bread	to serve

Preheat the oven to 425°F. Melt the butter in a saucepan over low heat. Cook the leek and garlic for 2 minutes, then add the shrimp and cook for 1–2 minutes or until just pink. Remove the shrimp with a slotted spoon and set aside.

Stir the flour into the pan and cook for 1 minute. Add the stock and wine, bring to a boil, and cook for 10 minutes or until most of the liquid has evaporated. Stir in the cream, bring to a boil, then reduce the heat and simmer for 20 minutes or until the liquid reduces by half. Stir in the lemon juice, herbs, and mustard.

Using half of the sauce, pour an even amount into each of four 1-cup ramekins. Divide the shrimp among the ramekins, then top with the remaining sauce.

Cut the pastry into four rounds, slightly larger than the rims of the ramekins. Put the pastry rounds over the shrimp mixture and press around the edges. Prick the pastry with a fork and brush with beaten egg. Bake for 20 minutes or until the pastry is crisp and golden. Serve with a salad and bread, if desired.

Thinly slice the white part of the leek

Cook the leek and garlic in the melted butter for 2 minutes

Add the stock and wine to the butter and leek mixture

creamy clam soup

serves 4

BIVALVE MOLLUSKS SUCH AS CLAMS MUST ALWAYS BE ALIVE WHEN COOKED. TO CHECK THIS, TIP THE SHELLS INTO A SINK FILLED WITH COLD WATER AND SORT THROUGH THEM—THEY SHOULD ALL BE CLOSED. IF ANY SHELLS ARE OPEN, TAP THEM ON THE SINK. IF THEY STAY OPEN, THROW THEM AWAY, AS THEY ARE DEAD.

clams	4 pounds, cleaned (see note)
butter	2 tablespoons
onion	1, chopped
celery	1 stalk, chopped
carrot	1 large, chopped
leek	1 large, sliced into rings
rutabaga	2 cups, diced
fish stock	3 1/4–4 cups
bay leaf	1
medium- or short-grain rice	a heaping 1/3 cup
cream	3/4 cup
Italian parsley	3 tablespoons finely chopped

Put the clams and 1 cup water in a large saucepan. Bring to a boil, then reduce the heat to medium and cover with a tight-fitting lid. Cook for 3–4 minutes or until the shells open. Strain into a bowl. Add enough fish stock to make up to 4 cups. Discard any clams that haven't opened. Remove all but eight of the clams from their shells.

Melt the butter in a clean saucepan. Add the vegetables and cook, covered, over medium heat for 10 minutes, stirring occasionally. Add the stock mixture and the bay leaf, bring to a boil, then reduce the heat and simmer for 10 minutes. Add the rice, return to a boil, cover, and cook over medium heat for 15 minutes or until the rice and vegetables are tender. Remove from the heat and stir in the clam meat. Remove the bay leaf and allow the mixture to cool for 10 minutes.

Purée the soup until smooth, then return to a clean saucepan. Stir in the cream, season, and gently reheat. Divide among four bowls and add the parsley and two reserved clams to each bowl.

Shellfish substitution—pipis

Note: Even if you have bought clams, mussels, pipis, or other bivalves as cleaned, put them in a bucket of seawater or heavily salted water for a couple of hours to ensure that they expel all their grit. Then rinse under cold running water and drain well.

Cook the clams in the water until they open

Remove the clam meat from the shells and set aside

japanese shrimp, scallop, and noodle soup .... serves 4

FRESH SCALLOPS ARE SUPERIOR TO FROZEN ONES, AND AVOID SUSPICIOUSLY PLUMP, PURE WHITE SPECIMENS; THEY MAY HAVE BEEN SOAKED IN WATER TO BULK THEM UP. SCALLOPS, UNLIKE MOST OTHER BIVALVES, DO NOT NEED TO BE SOAKED TO PURGE THEM; JUST RINSE THEM QUICKLY UNDER WATER TO REMOVE ANY SAND.

dried shiitake mushrooms	4
dried soba or somen noodles	3 1/2 ounces
bonito-flavored soup stock	1/4-ounce sachet
carrot	1 small, cut into thin batons
firm tofu	2/3 cup, cut into cubes
raw shrimp	16, peeled and deveined, tails intact
scallops	8, cleaned
scallions	2, finely chopped
mirin	1 tablespoon
shichimi togarashi	to serve (see note)

Soak the mushrooms in 1 1/4 cups boiling water for 30 minutes. Meanwhile, cook the noodles in a saucepan of boiling water for 2 minutes or until just tender, then drain and rinse with cold water. Return the noodles to the pan and cover.

In a large saucepan, mix the stock with 4 cups water. Drain the mushrooms and add the soaking liquid to the pan. Chop the mushroom caps, discarding the stalks. Add the mushrooms and carrot to the pan and bring the liquid to a boil. Reduce the heat to a simmer and cook for 5 minutes. Add the tofu, shrimp, scallops, scallions, and mirin to the pan. Cook at a gentle simmer for 4 minutes or until the shrimp have turned pink and are cooked and the scallops are firm and opaque.

Meanwhile, pour hot water over the noodles and swish them around to separate and warm them. Drain. Divide the noodles among four large bowls and pour the soup over them, dividing the seafood equally. Serve, offering the shichimi togarashi as a flavoring to sprinkle on top.

Fish substitution—chunks of firm white fish, fish balls

Note: Shichimi togarashi is a spicy Japanese condiment that can be found in the Asian section of some supermarkets.

Chop the caps of the soaked mushrooms, discarding the stalks

Cook the noodles in boiling water until just tender

Simmer gently until the shrimp are pink and the scallops opaque

three ways with batter

THE SECRET TO SUCCESSFUL DEEP FRYING IS TO HAVE THE OIL AT THE RIGHT TEMPERATURE. A DEEP-FRYING THERMOMETER IS HELPFUL HERE, OR YOU CAN SIMPLY GAUGE THE HEAT OF THE OIL BY PUTTING A CUBE OF WHITE BREAD INTO THE OIL AND SEEING HOW LONG IT TAKES TO BROWN. AT 315°F, IT WILL BROWN IN 30 SECONDS; AT 350°F, IT WILL TAKE 15 SECONDS; AND AT 375°F, 10 SECONDS. FOR SAFETY'S SAKE, ALWAYS LOWER FOODS GENTLY INTO THE OIL RATHER THAN DROPPING THEM IN.

beer-battered fish with crunchy fries

Cut 8 floury potatoes such as desiree, pontiac, or yellow finns into long 1/2-inch-wide fries, then soak them in cold water for 10 minutes. Drain and pat dry. Fill a deep fryer or large saucepan one-third full of oil and heat to 315°F. Cook the fries in batches for 4–5 minutes or until lightly golden. Remove with a slotted spoon and drain on crumpled paper towels. Pat dry 4 skinless firm white fish fillets such as cod, haddock, snapper, or perch, cut into strips, and dust with cornstarch. Make the batter at the last minute, as the bubbles in the beer help to make a better batter. To make the batter, sift 2/3 cup all-purpose flour into a large bowl and make a well in the center. Gradually pour in 3/4 cup beer, whisking to make a smooth batter. Dip the fillets into the batter and shake off any excess. Gently lower the fillets into the oil and deep-fry in batches for 5–7 minutes or until golden and cooked through. Turn with tongs if necessary. When cooked, the flesh should be moist and opaque. Drain on crumpled paper towels. Keep warm in an oven while you cook the fries a second time. Reheat the oil to 350°F. Cook the fries for 1–2 minutes, again in batches, until crisp and golden. Drain on crumpled paper towels. Serve the fish with the fries and lemon wedges. Serves 4.

fritto misto di mare

To make the batter, sift 1 2/3 cups all-purpose flour and 1/4 teaspoon salt into a bowl. Mix in 1/3 cup olive oil with a wooden spoon, then gradually add 1 1/4 cups tepid water, changing to a whisk when the mixture becomes liquid. Whisk until the batter is smooth and thick. Cover and leave to stand for 20 minutes in the refrigerator. Whisk 1 large egg white until stiff peaks form, then fold into the batter. This batter goes well with a range of seafood: 9-ounce cleaned baby calamari; 12 large shrimp, peeled and deveined, with tails intact; 8 cleaned small octopuses; 16 cleaned scallops; 12 fresh sardines, gutted and heads removed; and 9-ounce skinless fish fillets, cut into large cubes. To use, fill a deep fryer or a large saucepan one-third full of oil and heat to 375°F. Dry the seafood on paper towels. Working with one type of seafood at a time, dip it into the batter, shake off excess, then lower it into the oil, in batches if necessary. Deep-fry for 2–3 minutes or until golden and crisp. Drain on crumpled paper towels, then keep warm in a low oven while you cook the rest. Sprinkle with salt and serve with lemon wedges and a tartar sauce. Serves 4.

oyster po' boys

To make the batter, sift 1/2 cup self-rising flour, 1/4 teaspoon cayenne pepper, 1/4 teaspoon paprika, and a pinch of salt into a bowl. Beat 1 small egg and 1/2 cup milk together and gradually add to the flour, whisking to make a smooth batter. To use, fill a deep fryer or large saucepan one-third full of vegetable oil and heat to 350°F. Pat dry 18 freshly shucked oysters, dip into the batter, and deep-fry in batches for 1–2 minutes or until golden brown. Drain on crumpled paper towels and serve immediately, either as they are or sandwiched between crusty bread. Makes 18.

thai yellow fish and shrimp curry .... serves 4

MANY GOOD-QUALITY READY-MADE CURRY PASTES ARE AVAILABLE IN THE ASIAN SECTION OF MOST SUPERMARKETS. IF YOU'D PREFER TO USE ONE OF THESE RATHER THAN MAKE YOUR OWN, USE 3–4 TABLESPOONS OF YELLOW CURRY PASTE AND SKIP THE FIRST STEP.

curry paste

fresh turmeric	1 tablespoon chopped or
	2 teaspoons ground turmeric
ground coriander	1 teaspoon
ground cumin	1 teaspoon
yellow or red chilies	3 small
lemongrass	1 stem, cut into three pieces
fresh galangal or ginger	1 teaspoon grated
cilantro root	1 tablespoon chopped
garlic	2 large cloves, peeled
red Asian shallots	2, peeled
dried shrimp paste	1 teaspoon
oil	1/4 cup
coconut milk	3 1/4 cups
kaffir lime leaves	4, optional
lime	finely grated zest and juice of 1
fish sauce	1 tablespoon
palm sugar	1 teaspoon grated (soft brown sugar can be substituted)
Thai pea eggplants	30, optional (see note)
Thai or other baby eggplants (or regular eggplant)	4, quartered, or 2 1/3 cups, cut into small chunks
bean sprouts	3/4 cup, trimmed
jumbo shrimp	12, peeled and deveined, tails intact
lemon sole fillets	1 pound, 5 ounces, skinless and cut into bite-sized chunks
Thai basil or other basil leaves	2 tablespoons
cilantro leaves	1 tablespoon
steamed rice	to serve

To make the curry paste, put the turmeric, ground coriander, cumin, chilies, lemongrass, galangal, cilantro root, garlic, shallots, shrimp paste, and 1/4 cup water in a small food processor and blend until a thick paste forms. Alternatively, very finely chop all the ingredients with a sharp knife or pound in a mortar with a pestle and then mix everything together by hand.

Heat the oil in a large saucepan or wok and add the curry paste. Stirring often, cook for 5 minutes or until fragrant. Pour in the coconut milk, then add the lime leaves, lime zest and juice, fish sauce, sugar, Thai pea eggplants (if using), and other eggplant. Stir well, bring the mixture to a boil, then reduce the heat to low, cover with a lid, and simmer for 15 minutes or until the curry has thickened slightly and the eggplant is cooked.

Remove the lid from the pan and add the bean sprouts, shrimp, and chunks of fish. Cook for 4–5 minutes or until the shrimp have turned a pale pink and the fish is opaque. Stir in the basil and cilantro leaves, add a little salt if necessary, and serve with steamed rice.

Fish substitution—cod, hapuka, snapper, kingfish, grouper

Note: Pea eggplants are very small and round, about the size of a marble. They are sometimes available at Asian grocery stores.

Peel the ginger, then process with the other paste ingredients

Finely grate the zest of the lime, then juice it

jellyfish salad

serves 4

THIS TYPE OF RECIPE FALLS UNDER THE JAPANESE TITLE *AEMONO*, WHICH REFERS TO RECIPES IN WHICH INGREDIENTS ARE COATED IN A DRESSING OF SOME KIND. SERVE THIS SALAD AS A FIRST COURSE.

dried jellyfish	3 1/2 ounces, or a 5 1/2-ounce packet of ready-to-use jellyfish
firm tofu	2/3 cup
white sesame seeds	3 tablespoons, roasted and crushed
superfine sugar	2 teaspoons
sake	1 tablespoon
soy sauce	2 tablespoons
rice vinegar	2 tablespoons
cucumbers	1 1/2, peeled and cut into thin strips

If using dried jellyfish, put the jellyfish in a bowl and cover with boiling water. Leave to soak for 15 seconds, then drain. Return the jellyfish to the bowl and cover with warm water. Leave to soak for 3 hours, changing the water every hour. Finely slice using a sharp knife or scissors, then return to the soaking liquid and set aside until needed. If using a packet of ready-to-use jellyfish, follow the preparation instructions on the pack.

Place the tofu on a plate and cover with a clean dish towel. Place another plate on top with a weight, such as a can, on top of the plate. Leave the tofu to drain for 1 hour.

Tip away any excess liquid that has come out of the tofu and crumble the tofu into a coarse-meshed sieve set over a mixing bowl. Using a wooden spoon, push the tofu through the sieve into the bowl, then add 2 tablespoons of the sesame seeds, the sugar, sake, soy sauce, and rice vinegar. Mix until combined, then cover and chill until needed.

Strain the jellyfish, discarding the soaking liquid. Rinse and pat dry. Gently mix the jellyfish with the tofu dressing and cucumber strips. Serve garnished with the remaining sesame seeds.

Shellfish substitution—cooked shelled shellfish such as clams, small mussels, or small shrimp

If using dried jellyfish, first blanch it briefly in boiling water

Drain the jellyfish, then soak it in warm water until soft

Place a plate and can on top of the tofu and leave to drain

octopus salad .... serves 4

MANY RECIPES FOR OCTOPUS COME FROM MEDITERRANEAN COUNTRIES, WHERE THIS CEPHALOPOD IS PLENTIFUL. THIS RECIPE COMBINES TENDER SIMMERED OCTOPUS WITH TYPICAL MEDITERRANEAN FLAVORS TO PRODUCE A SIMPLE SALAD, PERFECT FOR A SUMMER LUNCH.

baby octopus	1 pound, 7 ounces, cleaned
mixed salad leaves	5 cups
lemon wedges	to serve

dressing

lemon juice	2 tablespoons
olive oil	½ cup
garlic	1 clove, thinly sliced
mint	1 tablespoon chopped
Italian parsley	1 tablespoon chopped
dijon mustard	1 teaspoon
cayenne pepper	a pinch

Bring a large saucepan of water to a boil and add the octopus. Simmer for 8–10 minutes or until the octopus is tender when tested with the point of a knife.

Meanwhile, make the dressing by mixing together the lemon juice, olive oil, garlic, mint, parsley, mustard, and cayenne pepper with some salt and freshly ground black pepper.

Drain the octopus well and put in a bowl. Pour the dressing over the top and cool for a few minutes before transferring to the refrigerator. Chill for at least 3 hours before serving on a bed of salad leaves. Drizzle a little of the dressing over the top and serve with lemon wedges.

The octopus has more often filled our imaginations than our stomachs. One species can grow to 30 feet from head to tentacle-tip and scientists have proven that octopuses are intelligent, with long- and short-term memories. So, perhaps it is not entirely surprising that many cooks are happier with baby octopus. Apart from size, the main difference between baby octopus and larger ones is the tenderness of the former; it needs neither beating nor blanching before cooking. Baby octopus can be cooked whole and are perfect for barbecuing and adding to salads. Japanese and Mediterranean cooks in particular make excellent use of these tender creatures.

three ways with oysters

TO CHECK THAT OYSTERS ARE FRESH AND ALIVE BEFORE COOKING THEM OR EATING THEM RAW, TAP ANY OPEN ONES AGAINST A SURFACE TO MAKE SURE THEY CLOSE; DISCARD ANY THAT DON'T. SCRUB OYSTERS WELL UNDER RUNNING WATER BEFORE USE, BUT DO NOT SOAK THEM. UNOPENED, LIVE OYSTERS CAN BE STORED FOR A WEEK; ONCE OPENED, STORE THEM IN THEIR LIQUID AND EAT WITHIN 24 HOURS. OYSTERS SHOULD OPEN ONCE THEY ARE COOKED; DISCARD ANY THAT REMAIN CLOSED. TO SHUCK OYSTERS, SEE THE NOTE BELOW.

oysters rockefeller

Arrange 24 freshly shucked oysters in their half shells on a bed of rock salt or crushed ice on a large platter. Cover and refrigerate until needed. Melt 1/4 cup butter in a saucepan. Add 2 finely chopped bacon slices and cook until browned. Add 8 finely chopped spinach leaves, 2 finely chopped scallions, 2 tablespoons finely chopped Italian parsley, 1/3 cup dry bread crumbs, and a drop of hot pepper sauce. Cook over medium heat until the spinach has wilted. Spoon onto the oysters and broil under high heat for 2–3 minutes or until golden. Transfer to a platter lined with rock salt and serve. Serves 4.

oysters with wasabi, soy, and ginger

Arrange 12 freshly shucked Pacific or other oysters in their half shells on a bed of rock salt or crushed ice on a large platter. Cover and refrigerate until needed. Mix together 1/3 teaspoon wasabi paste, 1 tablespoon dark soy sauce, 1 tablespoon rice wine vinegar, and 1 tablespoon finely chopped pink pickled ginger. Drizzle a little sauce over each oyster and serve. Serves 2.

oysters with ginger and lime

Arrange 12 freshly shucked oysters in their half shells on a bed of rock salt or crushed ice on a large platter. Cover and refrigerate until needed. Mix together 1/2 teaspoon finely grated fresh ginger, the zest and juice of 2 limes, 2 teaspoons Thai fish sauce, 1 tablespoon chopped cilantro leaves, and 2 teaspoons sugar. Drizzle a little sauce over each oyster and serve with lime wedges. Serves 2.

Note: Oysters should be opened, or shucked, just before they are to be used. To shuck oysters, you will need an oyster knife. Also, have ready a tray or platter thickly spread with crushed ice or rock salt, on which the opened oysters can be balanced so that they do not lose any of their flavorful juice. Place the oyster, curved side down, on a flat surface, with the hinged end facing you. Wrap the hand that will be grasping the oyster in a dish towel for protection. With the other hand, insert the blade of the oyster knife into the hinge of the oyster, twisting and pushing the knife to lever off the top shell (this will require quite a bit of force). Discard the top shell. Slip the oyster knife between the oyster and the bottom shell and sever the muscle that attaches the flesh to the shell. Carefully place the opened oyster in the prepared tray and remove any shell fragments. Do not wash the oyster, or you will wash away the precious juices. If eating oysters raw, it is custom to swallow them in one gulp, then to drink the delicious briny juices straight from the shell.

clams in coconut sauce.............................serves 4

THERE IS A BEWILDERING VARIETY OF EDIBLE CLAMS THROUGHOUT THE WORLD. THE SMALL SPECIES MAY BE EATEN RAW; LARGER ONES ARE BEST GROUND AND USED IN CHOWDERS. SMALL HARD-SHELL OR LITTLENECK CLAMS ARE PERFECT FOR THIS RECIPE.

French shallots	2, peeled
garlic	1 clove, peeled
lemongrass	2½-inch piece
small red chili	1
fresh ginger	1 teaspoon grated
candlenuts, unsalted macadamia nuts, or peanuts	1 tablespoon finely chopped
ground cumin	¾ teaspoon
ground coriander	1 teaspoon
palm sugar	1 teaspoon, grated (soft brown sugar can be substituted)
coconut milk	3¼ cups
oil	2 tablespoons
fish sauce	1 tablespoon
lime	juice of 1
fresh or dried coconut	¾ cup shredded
clams	3 pounds, 5 ounces small, cleaned

Put the shallots, garlic, lemongrass, chili, ginger, nuts, cumin, coriander, sugar, and ¼ cup of the coconut milk in a food processor and blend to a fine paste. Alternatively, chop all the ingredients finely and then blend by hand in a bowl. Heat the oil in a large saucepan and, when hot, add the paste. Stirring, cook for 5 minutes. Add the fish sauce, lime juice, the remaining coconut milk, and shredded coconut. Bring to a boil, then reduce to a simmer and cook uncovered for 10 minutes.

Meanwhile, put the clams in a separate large saucepan with ¼ cup water. Bring the water to a boil, then cover with a tight-fitting lid and cook over medium heat for 5–7 minutes or until the shells have opened. Drain, discarding the cooking liquid and any clams that have not opened. Add the clams to the coconut sauce. Mix and season with salt. Spoon the clams into four deep bowls and spoon the sauce over the top.

Shellfish substitution—cockles, pipis, mussels

Palm sugar is a dark, unrefined sugar obtained mostly from the sap of the palmyra palm tree. The sap is collected from the trees, boiled until it turns into a thick, dark syrup, then poured into molds—traditionally empty coconut shells—where it dries to form dense, heavy cakes. Palm sugar is widely used in sweet and savory dishes in India and Southeast Asia, particularly Thailand. It goes well with seafood such as salmon and shrimp. Buy in blocks or in jars from Asian stores and shave off the sugar as you need it. It is also known as jaggery or gur. Soft brown sugar can be substituted if palm sugar is unavailable.

seafood risotto... serves 4

RISOTTO RICE IS A SPECIAL TYPE THAT CAN ABSORB A LOT OF LIQUID AND STILL RETAIN ITS SHAPE. EAT RISOTTO AS SOON AS IT IS MADE; IT DOES NOT REHEAT WELL. ITALIANS OFTEN FORM LEFTOVER RISOTTO INTO LARGE BALLS, KNOWN AS *SUPPLI* OR *ARANCINI*, WHICH ARE CRUMBED AND FRIED, AND EATEN HOT OR COLD.

fish stock	7 cups
olive oil	2 tablespoons
onions	2, finely chopped
garlic	2 cloves, finely chopped
celery	1 stalk, finely chopped
risotto rice	2 cups
black mussels	8–10, cleaned
blue-eye cod fillet	5 1/2 ounces, cubed
raw shrimp	8, peeled and deveined, tails intact
Italian parsley	2 tablespoons chopped
oregano	1 tablespoon chopped
thyme	1 tablespoon chopped
butter	1 tablespoon
zest	of 1 lemon
lemon juice	1–2 teaspoons

Pour the stock into a saucepan and bring to a boil. Reduce the heat until just simmering, then cover.

Heat the olive oil in a large saucepan over medium heat. Add the onion, garlic, and celery and cook for 2–3 minutes. Add 2 tablespoons water, cover with a lid, and cook for 5 minutes or until the vegetables soften. Add the rice and, stirring constantly, cook over medium heat for 3–4 minutes or until the rice grains are well coated.

Gradually add 1/2 cup hot stock to the rice, stirring over low heat with a wooden spoon, until all the stock has been absorbed. Repeat, adding 1/2 cup stock each time until only a small amount of stock is left and the rice is just tender—this should take 20–25 minutes.

Meanwhile, bring 1/4 cup water to a boil in a saucepan. Add the mussels, cover with a lid, and cook for about 4–5 minutes, shaking the pan occasionally, until the mussels have opened. Drain and discard any unopened ones. If the mussels are large, remove them from their shells. Set the mussels aside until you're ready to add them to the risotto. Add the fish, shrimp, and the remaining hot stock to the rice and stir well. Cook for 5–10 minutes or until the seafood is just cooked and the rice is tender and creamy. Remove from the heat, add the mussels, cover, and set aside for 5 minutes. Stir the parsley, oregano, thyme, butter, lemon zest, and lemon juice through the risotto, then season to taste with salt and freshly ground black pepper. Leave to rest covered for a couple of minutes, then serve.

Fish substitution—coley, ling, cod

As each batch of liquid is absorbed, add a little more

Fold the seafood into the risotto and simmer until just cooked

three ways with mussels

MUSSELS HAVE BEEN CULTIVATED SINCE ANCIENT ROMAN TIMES. TO PREPARE MUSSELS, SCRUB THEM WELL UNDER RUNNING WATER TO REMOVE ANY BARNACLES AND PARASITES, AND PULL OFF THE FIBROUS "BEARD." DISCARD ANY MUSSELS THAT DO NOT CLOSE WHEN TAPPED; THESE ARE DEAD AND ARE NOT SAFE TO EAT. AS MUSSELS ARE INDISCRIMINATE FILTER FEEDERS, THEY CAN HARBOR HARMFUL ORGANISMS OR TOXINS FROM POLLUTED WATERS. IF YOU COLLECT YOUR OWN, MAKE SURE THEY COME FROM CLEAN WATERS.

mussels with coconut milk broth

Halve a lemongrass stalk and squash it a couple of times with the back of a wooden spoon. Grate a 2-inch piece of fresh ginger. Heat 2 tablespoons oil in a large saucepan and gently fry 1 finely chopped onion for 5 minutes. Add the lemongrass and ginger, 1 thinly sliced small red chili, $1^2/3$ cups canned coconut milk, and $3/4$ cup vegetable stock. Bring to a boil, then reduce the heat, cover, and simmer for 20 minutes. Remove the lemongrass, return the sauce to a boil, and add 3 pounds, 5 ounces cleaned mussels. Cover and cook, shaking the pan until the mussels open. Discard any unopened mussels and serve the mussels with the sauce spooned over. Serves 4.

mussels with tomato, garlic, and lemon

Heat 1 tablespoon oil in a large saucepan and gently fry 1 finely chopped onion and 2 crushed garlic cloves for 5 minutes. Add 1 pound, 2 ounces seeded and diced, firm, vine-ripened tomatoes, and 2 tablespoons lemon juice. Cook for 5 minutes, stirring gently occasionally. Add 3 pounds, 5 ounces cleaned mussels. Cover and cook, shaking the pan until the mussels open. Discard any unopened mussels. Serve the mussels with the grated zest from 1 large lemon and 2 tablespoons roughly chopped Italian parsley sprinkled over. Serves 4.

mussels with tangy bread crumbs and mayonnaise

Grate the zest from 1 lemon and squeeze the juice. Put $1/3$ cup good-quality mayonnaise into a bowl with 1 tablespoon of the lemon juice and 1 crushed garlic clove. Meanwhile, remove the crusts from 4 slices day-old crusty white bread. Put into a food processor and blend into bread crumbs. Transfer to a large frying pan and dry-fry until golden. Put into a bowl with the lemon zest and 2 tablespoons finely chopped cilantro leaves. Clean and debeard 2 pounds, 4 ounces black mussels. Bring $1/4$ cup white wine and 2 tablespoons water to a boil in a large saucepan. Add the mussels and cook, shaking the pan until the mussels open. Discard any unopened mussels. Remove the remaining mussels, shake off any excess liquid, and remove the top shell. Loosen the mussel from each shell. Spread each mussel with some of the mayonnaise and sprinkle with bread crumbs. Serve immediately. Serves 4 as an entrée.

paella

PAELLA IS PERHAPS THE QUINTESSENTIAL SPANISH DISH. ITS BASE IS RICE, SAFFRON, AND OLIVE OIL, BUT ARGUMENT CAN RAGE OVER WHAT OTHER INGREDIENTS—CHICKEN, SEAFOOD, SNAILS, PEAS, CHORIZO—SHOULD OR SHOULD NOT BE INCLUDED. WHAT IS INARGUABLE, HOWEVER, IS THAT IT IS DELICIOUS.

white wine	1/2 cup
red onion	1 small, chopped
black mussels	12–16, cleaned
olive oil	1/2 cup
chicken breast fillet	1 small, cut into bite-sized pieces
bacon slice	1, finely chopped
garlic	4 cloves, crushed
red bell pepper	1 small, finely chopped
red onion	1/2 small, finely chopped
vine-ripened tomato	1, peeled and chopped
chorizo	3 1/4 ounces, thinly sliced
cayenne pepper	a pinch
paella or short-grain rice	1 cup
saffron threads	1/4 teaspoon
chicken stock	2 cups, heated
peas	1/2 cup, fresh or frozen
raw shrimp	12, peeled and deveined
calamari	3 1/2 ounces, cleaned and cut into rings
cod fillets	3 1/2 ounces, skinned and cut into bite-sized pieces
Italian parsley	2 tablespoons chopped

Heat the wine and onion in a large saucepan. Add the mussels, cover, and gently shake the pan for 4–5 minutes over high heat. After 3 minutes, start removing opened mussels from the pan and set them aside. At the end of 5 minutes, discard any mussels that have not opened. Drain, reserving the liquid. Strain the liquid through a fine sieve lined with cheesecloth and reserve.

Heat half the oil in a large frying pan. Pat the chicken dry with paper towels, then cook the chicken for 5 minutes or until golden brown. Remove from the pan and set aside.

Heat the remaining oil in the pan, add the bacon, garlic, bell pepper, and extra red onion, and cook for 5 minutes or until the onion is softened but not browned. Add the tomato, chorizo, and cayenne pepper. Season with salt and freshly ground black pepper. Stir in the reserved cooking liquid, then add the rice and mix well.

Soak the saffron threads in 1/2 cup hot stock. Add this mixture and the remaining stock to the rice. Mix well. Bring slowly to a boil. Reduce the heat to low and simmer uncovered for 15 minutes, without stirring.

Put the peas, chicken, shrimp, calamari, and fish on top of the rice. Using a wooden spoon, push pieces of the seafood into the rice, cover, and cook over low heat for 10 minutes or until the rice is tender and the seafood is cooked. Add the mussels for the last 5 minutes to heat through. If the rice is not quite cooked, add a little extra stock and cook for a few more minutes. Leave to rest for 5 minutes, then sprinkle with parsley and serve.

Fish substitution—ling, mahimahi, blue-eye cod, monkfish

Soak the saffron threads in a small amount of hot stock

Arrange the peas, chicken, and seafood over the rice

steamed clams with corn and bacon..serves 4

IN NEW ENGLAND, CLAMBAKES ARE COOKED ON THE BEACH AT TIMES OF CELEBRATION. CLAMS AND OTHER SEAFOOD ARE BAKED, OFTEN ACCOMPANIED BY CORN ON THE COB. THIS RECIPE COMBINES CLAMS AND CORN WITH A FEW OTHER FLAVORS.

butter	1 tablespoon
onion	1 large, chopped
bacon	3^1/2 ounces, chopped
clams	3 pounds, 5 ounces, cleaned
corn	1 large cob, kernels removed
dry cider	^{2}/3 cup
heavy cream	^{2}/3 cup

Melt the butter in a large saucepan; when hot, add the onion and bacon. Cook over medium heat for about 5 minutes or until the onion is soft and the bacon cooked.

Tip the clams into a large saucepan with ^{1}/4 cup water and put over medium–high heat. Once the water is hot and the clams begin to steam, cover with a lid and cook for 2–3 minutes or until they have opened. Drain, reserving the liquid. Strain the liquid through a fine sieve lined with cheesecloth and reserve. Discard any clams that have not opened.

Add the corn kernels to the onion and bacon and cook for 3–4 minutes or until tender, stirring often. Pour in the cider and ^{1}/4 cup of the reserved cooking liquid. Bring to a boil, then simmer for 2 minutes. Stir in the cream and season with salt and freshly ground black pepper. Add the clams and toss them through the sauce. Serve in warmed deep bowls.

Shellfish substitution—pipis, cockles, mussels

Clams are bivalve mollusks, and are classed as either soft- or hard-shelled. Hard-shelled clams come in different sizes and colors, and most countries stick to their local favorites: the quahog (also called littleneck) is popular in the United States, palourde in France, hamaguri in Japan, and pipis, tuatua, and toheroa in Australasia. All are good raw or cooked. Soft-shelled clams, which have brittle shells that gape open, are most common in North America, home of the clambake. This great beachside feast normally features soft-shelled geoduck clams, which have long siphons. Clams must be bought live, then cleaned and shucked just before use.

three ways with calamari

THE GENERAL RULE WHEN COOKING CALAMARI AND OCTOPUS IS TO DO SO EITHER VERY BRIEFLY OR FOR A VERY LONG TIME—ANYTHING IN THE MIDDLE TENDS TO RESULT IN TOUGH MEAT. WHEN BUYING CALAMARI, READY-CLEANED CALAMARI TUBES ARE THE EASIEST OPTION. IF YOU WANT TO CLEAN AND PREPARE WHOLE CALAMARI OR OCTOPUS YOURSELF, SEE THE INSTRUCTIONS ON PAGE 127. SCORING A CRISSCROSS PATTERN ON THE INNER SURFACE OF CALAMARI TUBES CAUSES THEM TO CURL UP INTO ATTRACTIVE PINECONE SHAPES WHEN COOKED.

stir-fried calamari flowers with bell pepper

Halve lengthwise and open out 14 ounces calamari tubes. Wash off any soft jellylike substance and pat dry. Lay on a chopping board and score the inside of the flesh with a fine crisscross pattern, making sure not to cut all the way through. Cut the calamari into pieces that are about 1 1/4 x 2 inches. Blanch the calamari in a saucepan of boiling water for 25–30 seconds—each piece will curl up and the crisscross pattern will open out, hence the name "calamari flower." Remove and refresh in cold water, then drain and dry well. Heat a wok over high heat, add 1/4 cup oil, and heat until very hot. Add 2 tablespoons mashed, salted, and fermented black beans, 1 finely diced small onion, 1 finely diced small green bell pepper, 3–4 small slices peeled fresh ginger, 1 scallion cut into short lengths, and 1 chopped small red chili. Stir-fry for 1 minute. Add the calamari and 1 tablespoon Chinese rice wine, blend well, and stir for 1 minute. Sprinkle with 1/2 teaspoon roasted sesame oil. Serves 4 as part of a Chinese banquet or as a starter.

salt and pepper calamari

Halve lengthwise and open out 2 pounds, 4 ounces calamari tubes. Wash off any soft jellylike substance and pat dry. Lay on a chopping board and score the inside of the flesh with a fine crisscross pattern, making sure not to cut all the way through. Cut into pieces about 1 1/4 x 2 inches. Put in a flat nonmetallic dish and pour 1 cup lemon juice over the top. Cover and refrigerate for 15 minutes. Drain and pat dry. Combine 2 cups cornstarch, 1 1/2 tablespoons salt, 1 tablespoon ground white pepper, and 2 teaspoons superfine sugar in a bowl. Dip the calamari into 4 lightly beaten egg whites and then into the flour mixture, shaking off any excess. Fill a deep fryer or large saucepan one-third full of oil and heat to 350°F or until a cube of white bread dropped into the oil turns golden brown in 15 seconds. Cook batches of calamari for 1–2 minutes or until the flesh turns white and curls. Drain on crumpled paper towels. Serve with lemon wedges and garnish with cilantro leaves. Serves 6.

mediterranean calamari stew

Clean 2 pounds calamari (see page 127). Cut the body into rings and roughly chop the tentacles. (Alternatively, buy 1 pound cleaned calamari tubes.) Heat 2 tablespoons olive oil in a frying pan over medium heat. Add 1 chopped onion and cook for 5 minutes. Add 1 seeded and finely chopped red bell pepper and 2 crushed garlic cloves and cook for 2–3 minutes. Add 1/2 cup white wine, 1 pound, 5 ounces canned chopped tomatoes, and 1 tablespoon concentrated tomato purée. Bring to a boil. Stir in the calamari, reduce the heat, and simmer covered for 50 minutes. Add 1/2 cup pitted and halved black olives and a handful of Italian parsley leaves. Cook covered for an additional 10 minutes or until the calamari is tender. Serve with rice. Serves 4.

stir-fried calamari flowers with bell pepper

spaghetti alle vongole .... serves 4

VONGOLE IS SIMPLY THE ITALIAN WORD FOR CLAM. CLAMS VARY IN SIZE AND SHAPE FROM REGION TO REGION; ASK YOUR FISHMONGER FOR THE BEST LOCAL VARIETY. EVEN IF THEY ARE SOLD AS CLEANED, IT'S WORTH GIVING THEM AN EXTRA CLEAN YOURSELF: SEE PAGE 137 FOR INSTRUCTIONS ON HOW TO DO THIS.

olive oil	2 tablespoons
garlic	3 cloves, crushed
chili flakes	2 pinches
dry white wine	1/2 cup
canned chopped tomatoes	1 3/4 cups
Italian parsley	3 tablespoons finely chopped
clams	2 pounds, 4 ounces, cleaned
dried spaghetti or linguine	14 ounces
lemon zest	1/2 teaspoon grated
lemon halves	to serve

Heat the oil in a large, deep frying pan. Add the garlic and chili and cook over low heat for 30 seconds. Add the white wine, tomatoes, and 1 teaspoon of the parsley. Increase the heat and boil, stirring occasionally for 8–10 minutes or until the liquid is reduced by half.

Add the clams to the pan and cover with a lid. Shaking the pan often, increase the heat and cook for 3–5 minutes or until the clams open. Remove the clams from the pan, discarding any that have not opened. Stir in the remaining parsley and season. Boil the sauce for 3–4 minutes, until it is thick. Set half the clams aside and extract the meat from the rest.

Cook the pasta in a large saucepan of boiling salted water until al dente. Drain and stir through the sauce. Add the lemon zest, reserved clams, and clam meat. Toss well. Serve with the lemon halves.

Shellfish substitution—pipis, small mussels

Pasta is one of the world's great foods. Cheap, durable in its dried form, and endlessly versatile, it has been adopted by cooks the world over. The types and shapes of pasta are many: tiny stars, long strands or ribbons, large shells, and dozens more. Long thin pastas, which include spaghetti and linguine, are excellent for serving with simple sauces that will stick to their lengths without falling off, or with seafood such as clams, as the clams can be easily picked out and the flesh removed from the shells. Spaghetti alle vongole is a classic seafood and pasta combination; although, in fact, most shellfish is delicious with pasta.

moules marinières

A LA MARINIÈRE IS A FRENCH TERM DENOTING A DISH IN WHICH SEAFOOD, ESPECIALLY MUSSELS, IS COOKED IN WHITE WINE, USUALLY WITH ONIONS OR SHALLOTS. THE FOLLOWING IS A QUICK AND CLASSIC WAY TO PREPARE MUSSELS. SERVE THEM WITH PLENTY OF BREAD TO SOP UP THE DELICIOUS JUICES.

butter	2 tablespoons
onion	1 large, chopped
celery	1/2 stalk, chopped
garlic	2 cloves, crushed
white wine	1 2/3 cups
bay leaf	1
thyme	2 sprigs
mussels	4 pounds, 8 ounces, cleaned (see page 173)
heavy cream	1 cup
Italian parsley	2 tablespoons chopped
crusty bread	to serve

Melt the butter in a large saucepan over medium heat. Add the onion, celery, and garlic. Stirring occasionally, cook for about 5 minutes or until the onion is softened but not browned.

Add the wine, bay leaf, and thyme to the saucepan and bring to a boil. Add the mussels, cover the pan tightly, and simmer over low heat for 2–3 minutes, shaking the pan occasionally. With tongs, lift out the mussels as they open and put them into a warm dish. Discard any mussels that haven't opened after 3 minutes.

Strain the cooking liquid through a cheesecloth-lined fine sieve into a clean saucepan to remove any grit or sand. Bring the liquid to a boil and boil for 2 minutes. Add the cream and reheat without boiling. Season well. Serve the mussels in individual bowls with the liquid poured over. Sprinkle with the parsley and serve with plenty of bread.

As the mussels open, remove them and place in a warmed dish

Strain the liquid through a sieve lined with cheesecloth into a clean pan

three ways with scallops

SCALLOPS ARE FOUND IN ALL SEAS. THE MANY SPECIES CAN ALL BE COOKED IN THE SAME WAYS, OR EATEN RAW. ALL HAVE FAN-SHAPED SHELLS, WHITE MEAT, AND EDIBLE ORANGE-RED ROE. IF BOUGHT OPENED BUT STILL ON THE HALF SHELL, THEY WILL NEED TO BE RINSED, AS THEY CAN BE SANDY. IF BOUGHT WHOLE, THEY WILL NEED TO BE SCRUBBED. DISCARD ANY THAT ARE OPEN BUT DO NOT CLOSE QUICKLY WHEN SHARPLY TAPPED. ONCE COOKED, THE SHELLS SHOULD OPEN UP; DISCARD ANY THAT REMAIN CLOSED.

scallop ceviche

Clean 16 scallops in their closed shells by scrubbing under running water. One by one, hold the scallop in a dish towel and, with a sharp knife or an oyster knife, carefully pry open the shell. Lift off the top shell and loosen the scallop from the shell. Pull off and discard the scallop's outer gray fringe and outer membrane. Retain the shells. In a nonmetallic bowl, mix together 1 teaspoon finely grated lime zest, 1/4 cup lime juice, 2 chopped garlic cloves, 2 seeded and chopped red chilies, 1 tablespoon chopped cilantro leaves, and 1 tablespoon olive oil. Season with salt and freshly ground black pepper. Put the scallops in the dressing and stir to coat. Cover with plastic wrap and refrigerate for 2 hours; the acid in the lime juice will "cold-cook" the scallop flesh. To serve, slide each scallop back onto a half shell and spoon a little of the lime dressing over it. Top each scallop with a whole cilantro leaf. Serve cold. Serves 4.

scallops in black bean sauce

Clean 24 scallops in their closed shells by scrubbing under running water. Heat 1 tablespoon oil in a wok and, when hot, add the scallops. Cook for 2 minutes or until just firm. (Do not overcook or they will be tough and rubbery.) Transfer to a plate. Mix together 1 tablespoon soy sauce, 2 tablespoons Chinese rice wine, 1 teaspoon sugar, and 1 tablespoon water. Set aside. Add an additional 1 tablespoon oil to the wok and heat until it is beginning to smoke. Add 1 finely chopped garlic clove, 1 finely chopped scallion, and 1/2 teaspoon finely grated fresh ginger. Cook for 30 seconds. Add 1 tablespoon salted, fermented black beans that have been rinsed and drained, and the reserved soy sauce mixture. Bring to a boil. Return the scallops to the sauce with 1 teaspoon roasted sesame oil and allow to simmer for about 30 seconds. Serve immediately with rice and steamed Asian greens. Serves 4.

Shellfish substitution—shrimp, crayfish or lobster, baby calamari

barbecued asian-style scallops

Place 10 1/2 ounces scallop meat in a shallow nonmetallic bowl. In a separate bowl, combine 1/3 cup sweet chili sauce, 1 teaspoon fish sauce, 2 teaspoons lime juice, and 1 teaspoon peanut oil. Pour the mixture over the scallop meat and mix gently to coat. Allow to marinate for 1 hour. Drain the seafood well and reserve the marinade. Preheat a barbecue or flatplate to high, add 1 tablespoon peanut oil, and heat. Cook the scallops for 3–5 minutes or until tender. Drizzle with a little of the leftover marinade during cooking. Serve on a bed of steamed rice with wedges of lime. Serves 2.

laksa lemak ...... serves 4

A ROBUSTLY FLAVORED SOUP, LAKSA IS A MEAL IN ITSELF. IT FEATURES RICE NOODLES, SEAFOOD OR CHICKEN, AND VARIOUS GARNISHES IN A SPICY STOCK. LAKSA LEMAK, THE SINGAPOREAN VERSION, IS RICH WITH COCONUT MILK AND IS THE MOST POPULAR TYPE.

rice noodles	2³/₄ cups
unsalted macadamias	¹/₂ cup
oil	1 tablespoon
canned coconut milk	3¹/₄ cups
lime juice	¹/₃ cup
bean sprouts	1²/₃ cups, trimmed
large raw shrimp	20, peeled and deveined
large scallops	16, cleaned
Vietnamese mint	a handful, shredded, with a few left whole to garnish
short cucumber	¹/₂, peeled and thinly sliced

paste

red chilies	3, seeded and chopped
lemongrass	2 stems
fresh ginger	1 teaspoon grated
red Asian shallots	4, peeled
shrimp paste	1 tablespoon
ground turmeric	1 tablespoon

Soak the rice noodles in boiling water for 10 minutes. Drain.

To make the paste, put all the paste ingredients and 1 tablespoon water into a food processor and blend until smooth. Alternatively, finely chop by hand and mix well.

In a saucepan, dry-fry the nuts over medium heat until golden, shaking the pan often. Transfer to a plate.

Heat the oil in the same saucepan, add the prepared paste, and cook over medium heat for 2 minutes. Stir in the coconut milk, then gently simmer for 10 minutes or until it thickens slightly. Roughly chop the nuts.

When the coconut milk mixture is ready, add the lime juice and three-quarters of the bean sprouts to the pan. Season with salt, bring back to a simmer, then add the shrimp and scallops and cook for about 5 minutes or until the shrimp have turned pink. Add the shredded mint and the noodles. Mix the whole mint leaves with the chopped nuts and cucumber.

Ladle into four deep bowls, then sprinkle with the remaining bean sprouts and the mint and cucumber mixture.

Fish substitution—cubes of any firm-fleshed white fish

Soak the rice noodles in boiling water to soften them

Stir the coconut milk into the fried spice paste

spaghetti with seafood .... serves 4

SEAFOOD PASTA IN MANY RESTAURANTS AROUND THE WORLD IS ERRONEOUSLY TERMED *MARINARA*. MARINARA IS TRADITIONALLY THE SAUCE MADE BY ITALIAN FISHERMEN OR THEIR WIVES, TO WHICH THE DAY'S CATCH WOULD BE ADDED. SO THE NAME, IN FACT, REFERS TO THE SAUCE, NOT THE SEAFOOD.

tomato sauce

olive oil	2 tablespoons
onion	1, finely chopped
carrot	1, finely chopped
garlic	2 cloves, crushed
canned chopped tomatoes	1³/₄ cups
white wine	¹/₂ cup
sugar	1 teaspoon
white wine	¹/₄ cup
fish stock	¹/₄ cup
garlic	1 clove, crushed
black mussels	12, cleaned, optional
clams	14 ounces, cleaned, or 7 ounces canned, drained
spaghetti	13 ounces
butter	1 tablespoon
calamari tubes	4¹/₂ ounces, cleaned and cut into rings
cod fillet	4¹/₂ ounces, skinned and cut into bite-sized pieces
raw shrimp	7 ounces, peeled and deveined, tails left on
Italian parsley	a large handful, chopped

To make the tomato sauce, heat the oil in a saucepan, add the onion and carrot, and cook over medium heat for 10 minutes or until lightly browned. Add the garlic, tomato, white wine, and sugar, bring to a boil, then reduce the heat and gently simmer for 30 minutes, stirring occasionally.

Heat the wine, stock, and garlic in a large saucepan. Add the mussels and clams (if using clams in the shell). Cover and shake the pan over high heat for 5 minutes. After 3 minutes, start removing any opened mussels and clams and set them aside. After a total of 5 minutes, discard any unopened mussels and clams. Strain the cooking liquid through a fine sieve lined with cheesecloth and reserve.

Cook the spaghetti in a large saucepan of boiling salted water until al dente. Drain and keep warm.

Meanwhile, melt the butter in a frying pan and stir-fry the calamari, cod, and shrimp in batches for 2 minutes or until just cooked. Remove from the heat and add to the tomato sauce, along with the reserved cooking liquid, mussels, parsley, and clams (in the shell or canned). Gently heat through, then toss the sauce with the pasta and serve.

Fish substitution—haddock, flounder, or any firm white fish

Add the garlic, tomato, wine, and sugar to the carrot and onion

Fry the calamari, cod, and shrimp in batches in the melted butter

Add the seafood and remaining ingredients to the tomato sauce

the perfect mussel

Mussels are bivalve mollusks that are stored and cooked live. Once they die they deteriorate rapidly, so care should be taken in storing and cooking them. The best practice is to put them in a bowl and cover with a damp dish towel—do not store them in water, as they will die. Keep them in the bottom of the refrigerator, preferably in the salad compartment, at around 35°F. They should last a couple of days like this, but it is preferable to eat them on the day of purchase.

Mussels must be cleaned well before cooking, as they are filter feeders and hence can be quite gritty. Put the mussels in a sinkful of cold water and clean them one by one. Using a small sharp knife, remove any barnacles and pull away the hairy "beard." This is what the mussel uses to hang on to the rock or rope when growing. Discard any mussels with broken shells. Tap open mussels on the work surface to close them. If they do not close, they are probably dead, so discard them. You may also want to discard any particularly heavy ones, as they may be full of sand, which will affect your finished dish. Once cleaned, rinse the mussels one or two more times and cook as soon as possible after cleaning. Once again, do not store them in water if not cooking immediately.

The best way to cook mussels is to steam them open in a large saucepan. Bring about $1/2$ inch water, white wine, or other cooking liquid to a boil, stirring through any other flavorings, such as garlic, onion, or herbs. Add the mussels, cover tightly with the lid, and cook for a couple of minutes, shaking the pan regularly. Remove those mussels that have opened, then cook for another minute to open the rest. Discard any mussels that do not open, as they are probably dead. Eat the mussels immediately, with or without the cooking liquid.

marmite dieppoise .... serves 6

THE USE OF CIDER AND CREAM IN THIS RICH SEAFOOD STEW REVEALS ITS ORIGINS IN THE FRENCH REGION OF NORMANDY. TRADITIONALLY TURBOT AND SOLE ARE USED, BUT SALMON ADDS A SPLASH OF COLOR. THE DISH TAKES ITS NAME FROM THE IRON OR EARTHENWARE POT IN WHICH IT IS TRADITIONALLY COOKED.

salmon fillet	10½-ounce, skinless
sole fillet	14-ounce, skinless
cider or dry white wine	1¾ cups
mussels	16, cleaned
butter	2 tablespoons
garlic	1 clove, crushed
French shallots	2, finely chopped
celery	2 stalks, finely chopped
leek	1 large, white part only, thinly sliced
small chestnut mushrooms	4 cups, sliced
large raw shrimp	12, peeled and deveined
bay leaf	1
heavy cream	1¼ cups
Italian parsley	3 tablespoons finely chopped

Cut the salmon fillet into bite-sized chunks and cut the sole into thick strips widthwise. Set aside until needed.

Pour the cider or white wine into a large saucepan and bring to a simmer. Add the mussels, cover, and cook for 3–5 minutes, shaking the pan occasionally. Put a fine sieve over a large bowl and tip the mussels into the sieve. Transfer the mussels to a plate, throwing away any that haven't opened during cooking. Line the sieve with cheesecloth and strain the cooking liquid again to get rid of any grit or sand.

Add the butter to the cleaned saucepan and melt over moderate heat. Add the garlic, shallot, celery, and leek. Stirring occasionally, cook for 7–10 minutes or until the vegetables are just soft. Add the mushrooms and cook for an additional 4–5 minutes or until softened. While the vegetables are cooking, remove the mussels from their shells. You may want to save six mussels to use as a garnish.

Add the strained cooking liquid and the bay leaf to the vegetables in the saucepan and bring to a simmer. Add the salmon, sole, and shrimp and cook for 3–4 minutes or until the fish is opaque and the shrimp have turned pink. Stir in the cream and cooked mussels and simmer gently for 2 minutes. Season to taste and stir in the parsley. Divide among six bowls and garnish each with a reserved mussel, if you wish.

Remove the fibrous beards from the mussels

Steam the mussels in the cider or wine until they open

Remove the mussel meat from the shells

gumbo .... serves 6

A SPECIALTY OF THE CAJUN CUISINE OF LOUISIANA, GUMBO IS A CROSS BETWEEN A SOUP AND A STEW. ITS BASE IS A DARK ROUX, A SLOWLY COOKED AND BROWNED AMALGAM OF FLOUR AND OIL OR LARD, WHICH IS WHAT GIVES IT SUCH RICH FLAVOR AND COLOR.

roux

oil	1/3 cup
all-purpose flour	a scant 2/3 cup
onion	1, finely chopped
raw crabs	4, cleaned (see page 124)
chorizo sausage	1 pound, cut into bite-sized pieces
scallions	6, sliced
green bell pepper	1, roughly chopped
Italian parsley	3 tablespoons chopped
chili powder	1/4 teaspoon
shrimp	1 pound, 2 ounces, peeled and deveined
oysters	24, freshly shucked
long-grain rice	1 1/2 tablespoons
filé powder	1/2 teaspoon (see note)

To make the roux, pour the oil into a large heavy-based saucepan over low heat. Gradually add the flour, stirring after each addition, to make a thin roux. Continue to cook and stir over a low heat for 35 minutes or until it turns dark brown. Add the onion and cook for 4 minutes or until tender. Gradually pour in 6 cups boiling water, continually stirring to dissolve the roux, and bring to a simmer.

Cut the crabs into small pieces. Add the crab, sausage, scallion, bell pepper, parsley, and chili powder to the roux. Cook for 30 minutes, then add the shrimp and oysters and their juices, and cook for another 5 minutes or until the shrimp are pink.

Cook the rice in salted boiling water for about 10 minutes or until just cooked through. Put a couple of tablespoons of rice in the bottom of each serving bowl.

Just before you are ready to serve the gumbo, season it with salt and freshly ground black pepper, then stir in the filé powder. Do not reheat after the filé is added, or the gumbo will become stringy. Ladle the gumbo over the rice in the bowls and serve at once.

Note: Filé powder is a flavoring and thickening agent often used in Creole and Cajun cooking. It is made by drying and then grinding sassafras leaves. Look for it in specialty food stores or in specialty herb stores.

Stir the flour into the oil and cook over low heat for 35 minutes

Gradually add boiling water to the roux

Continually stir the mixture to dissolve the roux

sea urchin roe with spaghetti and gremolata .... serves 4

MANY SEA URCHIN SPECIES ARE FOUND AROUND THE WORLD. MOST OFTEN, IT IS THE ORANGE ROE THAT ARE EATEN. THEY ARE AT THEIR BEST WHEN RIPE, JUST BEFORE BREEDING. SEA URCHIN ROE ARE TRADITIONALLY SERVED RAW, ACCOMPANIED BY MERELY A SQUEEZE OF FRESH LEMON JUICE.

olive oil	¼ cup
French shallots	2, finely chopped
spaghetti	18 ounces
lemon zest	1 tablespoon finely grated
Italian parsley	2 tablespoons finely chopped
sea urchin	the roe of 6

Heat the olive oil in a frying pan and, when hot, add the shallot. Cook over medium heat for 5 minutes, stirring occasionally, until softened and lightly browned.

Cook the spaghetti in a saucepan of boiling salted water until al dente. Drain and return to the pan.

To make the gremolata, combine the lemon zest and parsley. Add with the oil and shallots to the pasta. Season with salt and ground black pepper, and toss together. Serve in large, warm, shallow bowls with the sea urchin roe arranged over the top.

The unusual-looking sea urchin is best described by explaining that the word *urchin* comes from the old English word for hedgehog. Hidden inside this protective armory are five orange roe (corals), considered a delicacy in France and Japan. To open a sea urchin, cut a round piece out of the top of the shell (the end opposite the mouth) with kitchen scissors. Lift off the piece of shell and drain any juices. Carefully scoop out the roe. They can be eaten as they are, with lemon juice; incorporated into omelets; or added to creamy sauces to serve with fish. The Japanese also make an expensive sea urchin paste.

zanzibar pilaf with calamari and shrimp . . . . serves 4

THE LEGACY LEFT BY ARAB TRADERS IS CLEAR IN THE AVAILABILITY AND POPULARITY OF SO MANY WONDERFUL SPICES IN ZANZIBAR, A BEAUTIFUL ARCHIPELAGO IN THE INDIAN OCEAN, OFF THE COAST OF TANZANIA. THIS AROMATIC RICE DISH IS REDOLENT OF THOSE RICH, WARM FLAVORS.

cinnamon	1 stick
cloves	6
cardamom	6 pods
coriander seeds	1/2 teaspoon
black peppercorns	1/2 teaspoon
oil	3 tablespoons
onions	2 large, finely chopped
garlic	3 cloves, finely chopped
ginger	2 teaspoons finely chopped
basmati rice	1 1/4 cups
vegetable stock	2 1/3 cups
tomatoes	3, chopped
raisins	1 2/3 cups
baby calamari	1 pound, cleaned, tentacles left intact
raw shrimp	1 pound, peeled and deveined, tails left on

Place the cinnamon, cloves, cardamom pods, coriander seeds, and black peppercorns in a large cup or mug and cover with about 1 1/4 cups hot water. Leave to infuse for at least 30 minutes.

Heat 2 tablespoons of the oil in a large sauté or frying pan, add the onion, and cook over medium heat for 10 minutes, stirring occasionally until softened. Add the garlic and ginger and cook, stirring, for an additional 2 minutes. Add the rice and stir to coat with the oil. Add the spices, their liquid, and the stock, and bring to a boil. Then reduce the heat, cover the pan, and cook for 5 minutes, stirring occasionally. Add the tomatoes and raisins, cover again, and, stirring occasionally, cook for an additional 8–10 minutes or until the rice is tender. If the rice appears to be drying out, add a little more boiling water. Season to taste, then remove the pan from the heat.

Remove the calamari tentacles from where they join the body. Reserve. Cut the calamari tubes open. Using a sharp knife, score a fine crisscross pattern on the inside of each tube, careful not to cut all the way through the tubes. Halve or quarter the tubes.

Season the shrimp and calamari thoroughly with salt and pepper. Heat the remaining tablespoon of oil in a frying pan and cook the shrimp for 2–3 minutes. Pile the pilaf onto a serving dish and place the shrimp on top. Quickly cook the calamari in the frying pan for 30–60 seconds on each side, adding a little more oil if necessary. Place on top of the pilaf and serve.

Pour boiling water over the spices and allow them to infuse

Add the spices, their liquid, and the stock to the rice

asian shrimp and noodle salad . . . . serves 4

THIS DISH IS THE WORK OF MINUTES, YET IS SUBSTANTIAL AND DELICIOUS. SIMPLIFY IT EVEN FURTHER BY BUYING COOKED, PEELED SHRIMP. KECAP MANIS IS AN INDONESIAN MARINADE, FLAVORING, AND CONDIMENT. IT RESEMBLES SOY SAUCE, BUT IS THICKER AND SWEETER, AND USUALLY CONTAINS STAR ANISE AND GARLIC.

dressing

ginger	2 tablespoons, grated
soy sauce	2 tablespoons
sesame oil	2 tablespoons
red wine vinegar	1/3 cup
sweet chili sauce	1 tablespoon
garlic	2 cloves, crushed
kecap manis	1/3 cup
dried instant egg noodles	4 cups
cooked large shrimp	1 pound, 2 ounces, peeled and deveined, tails intact
scallions	5, sliced on the diagonal
cilantro	2 tablespoons chopped
red bell pepper	1, diced
snow peas	1 1/4 cups, cut into halves
lime wedges	to serve

For the dressing, whisk together the ginger, soy sauce, sesame oil, vinegar, chili sauce, garlic, and kecap manis in a large bowl.

Cook the egg noodles in a large saucepan of boiling water for 2 minutes or until tender, then drain thoroughly. Cool in a large serving bowl.

Add the dressing, shrimp, scallions, cilantro, bell pepper, and snow peas to the noodles and toss gently. Serve with the lime wedges.

Although fresh ginger does not look like much, this knobbly, beige-colored, tropical rhizome is indispensable in much seafood cooking due to its pungent and cleansing flavor. Fresh ginger is a classic ingredient in Chinese steamed fish dishes, Japanese broths, and Indian spice pastes and rubs for fish, and it is a more than equal partner for the rich ingredients used in fish stews and soups, such as coconut milk, chili, nuts, and cilantro. Store fresh ginger tightly wrapped in plastic wrap in the refrigerator; peel and chop or grate before using. Ginger is also available in powdered, dried, pickled, crystallized, or preserved forms.

seafood lasagna .... serves 6

LASAGNA, A CLASSIC COMFORT FOOD, WORKS EQUALLY WELL WITH SEAFOOD AS WITH MEAT, WITH THE BONUS THAT A SEAFOOD SAUCE TAKES MUCH LESS TIME TO COOK THAN ITS MEAT COUNTERPART.

olive oil	1 tablespoon
butter	1 tablespoon
onion	1, finely chopped
garlic	2 cloves, crushed
small raw shrimp	14 ounces, peeled and deveined
skinless firm white fish fillets	1 pound, 2 ounces, cut into 3/4-inch pieces
scallops	9 ounces, with roe, cleaned
canned diced tomatoes	3 1/2 cups
concentrated tomato purée	2 tablespoons
soft brown sugar	1 teaspoon
cheddar cheese	1/2 cup grated
Parmesan cheese	1/4 cup grated
fresh lasagna sheets	9 ounces
salad	to serve

cheese sauce

butter	1/2 cup
all-purpose flour	2/3 cup
milk	6 cups
cheddar cheese	2 cups grated
Parmesan cheese	1 cup grated

Preheat the oven to 350°F. Grease a 10 3/4 x 8 1/4-inch, 10-cup ovenproof dish.

Heat the oil and butter in a large saucepan. Add the onion and cook for 2–3 minutes or until softened but not browned. Add the garlic and cook for 30 seconds or until fragrant. Add the shrimp and fish pieces and cook for 2 minutes before adding the scallops. Cook for an additional minute. Stir in the tomatoes, concentrated tomato purée, and sugar. Simmer for 5 minutes.

Combine the grated cheddar and Parmesan cheeses in a bowl and set aside until needed for topping the lasagna.

To make the cheese sauce, melt the butter over low heat in a saucepan, then stir in the flour and cook for 1 minute or until the mixture is pale and foaming. Remove the pan from the heat and gradually stir in the milk. Return the pan to the heat and stir until the sauce boils and thickens. Reduce the heat, simmer for 2 minutes, then stir in the cheddar and Parmesan cheeses. Season to taste with salt and freshly ground black pepper.

Line the ovenproof dish with a layer of lasagna sheets. Spoon half of the seafood sauce over the lasagna sheets. Arrange another layer of lasagna sheets over the top. Top with half of the cheese sauce. Repeat with more lasagna sheets, the remaining seafood sauce, a final layer of lasagna sheets, and the remaining cheese sauce. Then sprinkle the top with the combined cheddar and Parmesan cheeses. Bake for 30 minutes or until the top is golden. Leave for 10 minutes to firm up before slicing. Serve with a salad.

Fish substitution—hake, snapper, flake, gemfish, ling

Stir the flour into the melted butter and cook for 1 minute

Add the milk and cook, stirring, until the sauce thickens

matelote normande .... serves 4

MATELOTE IS THE NAME TRADITIONALLY GIVEN TO A FISH STEW, ESPECIALLY ONE CONTAINING EEL. ITS NAME IS DERIVED FROM THE FRENCH WORD FOR SAILOR, *MATELOT*. THIS VERSION USES CIDER, WHICH IS MADE AND COMMONLY USED FOR COOKING IN THE NORMANDY REGION OF FRANCE.

mixed firm white fish fillets, such as turbot or cod steaks	1 pound, 9 ounces, skinless
olive oil	1/3 cup
white bread	2 slices, crusts removed, cut into cubes
butter	1/3 cup, softened
French shallots or button onions	8, cut in halves if large
button mushrooms	3²/3 cups, cut in halves or quarters if large
garlic	1 large clove, finely chopped
large scallops	8, white meat and roe separated
dry cider	1²/3 cups
bouquet garni	1
flour	1 tablespoon
heavy cream	²/3 cup
Italian parsley	2 tablespoons finely chopped

Cut the fish into bite-sized chunks and set aside. Preheat the oven to 275°F. To make the croutons, heat ¼ cup oil in a large frying pan. When hot, add the bread in batches and fry for 2 minutes or until golden brown, stirring as they cook so the croutons brown evenly. Drain on paper towels.

Melt 1 tablespoon of the butter and the remaining oil in the frying pan. When hot, add the shallots. Cook for 5 minutes over medium heat, then add the mushrooms and cook for 10 minutes, stirring occasionally. When cooked, put in a dish, cover with foil, and keep warm.

Meanwhile, melt another tablespoon of the butter in a large sauté pan and, when hot, add the garlic. Cook for 30 seconds, then reduce the heat and add the fish (not the scallops) and cook for 2–3 minutes on each side, turning occasionally.

Cut the white scallop meat in half widthwise. Add the cider and bouquet garni to the fish, bring to a simmer, and add the white scallop meat. Cook gently for 2 minutes. Add the scallop roe and cook for an additional minute. Remove all the seafood from the liquid and keep warm.

Blend the remaining butter with the flour in a cup to make a paste. Bring the cider mixture to a boil and whisk in the butter and flour paste to the liquid, bit by bit, and allow the sauce to thicken. Simmer for 1 minute, then stir the cream into the sauce. Heat through and season to taste.

Return the seafood to the pan. Remove the bouquet garni. Serve with the shallots, button mushrooms, croutons, and parsley.

Fish substitution—rock salmon (huss), halibut, or any other firm white fish

Fry the bread in the oil until golden brown on all sides

Whisk the butter and flour paste into the cider mixture

moqueca de peixe .... serves 4

THIS IS A SIMPLE, DELICIOUS SEAFOOD STEW FROM THE PROVINCE OF BAHIA IN THE NORTHEAST OF BRAZIL. THE COOKING OF THE REGION HAS BEEN HEAVILY INFLUENCED BY THE PORTUGUESE AND BY THE HUGE NUMBER OF SLAVES THAT THEY BROUGHT WITH THEM FROM GUINEA AND SUDAN IN THE EARLY NINETEENTH CENTURY.

fish steaks such as mahimahi, bream, or halibut	4 x 7-ounce
raw shrimp	8 large, peeled and deveined
lime juice	1/4 cup
olive oil	2 tablespoons
onion	1 large, finely chopped
garlic	4 large cloves, crushed
red bell pepper	1 large, seeded and chopped
habanero chili	1, seeded and finely chopped
vine-ripened tomatoes	1 pound, 2 ounces
coconut milk	1 1/4 cups
cilantro leaves	3 tablespoons chopped

Put the fish and shrimp in a shallow nonmetallic dish. Drizzle the lime juice over the fish. Season with salt and freshly ground black pepper and turn the fish in the juice. Cover and leave for 30 minutes in the refrigerator.

Meanwhile, heat the oil in a large saucepan and add the onion. Cook for 8–10 minutes or until softened, then add the garlic, bell pepper, and chili. Cook for an additional 3 minutes, stirring occasionally.

Score a cross in the base of each tomato. Put into boiling water for 20 seconds, then plunge into cold water. Drain and peel the skin away from the cross. Chop the tomatoes, discarding the cores and seeds.

Add the tomato to the pan and cook for 10 minutes. Allow to cool slightly, then tip the sauce into a food processor or blender and blend until smooth. Alternatively, push the mixture through a coarse sieve or mouli by hand. Return the sauce to the pan. Add the coconut milk and bring to a gentle simmer. Lift the fish and the shrimp out of the dish and add to the pan, leaving behind any remaining marinade. Cook for 4 minutes or until opaque. Season to taste with salt and freshly ground black pepper, and sprinkle with cilantro over the top.

Fish substitution—sole, cod, bass

Score a cross in the base of each tomato

Plunge the tomato into cold water to stop further cooking

Peel the skin away from the cross and discard

index

Thunder Bay Press
An imprint of the Advantage Publishers Group
5880 Oberlin Drive, San Diego, CA 92121-4794
www.thunderbaybooks.com

Library of Congress Cataloging-in-Publication Data
Knudsen, Kathy.
    Cooking seafood / [Kathy Knudsen].
      p. cm.
    ISBN 1-59223-429-1 (pbk.)
    1. Cookery (Seafood)   I. Title.

TX747.S3648 2005
641.6'92--dc22

2005047276

Printed in China.
1 2 3 4 5   09 08 07 06 05

IMPORTANT: Those who might be at risk from the effects of salmonella poisoning (the elderly, pregnant women, young children, and those suffering from immune deficiency diseases) should consult their doctor with any concerns about eating raw eggs.

CONVERSION GUIDE: You may find cooking times vary depending on the oven you are using. For convection ovens, as a general rule, set the oven temperature to 70°F lower than indicated in the recipe.

Chief Executive: Juliet Rogers
Publisher: Kay Scarlett
Concept and art direction: Vivien Valk
Designer: Lauren Camilleri
Editorial director: Diana Hill
Project manager and editor: Janine Flew
Text: Margaret Malone, Katy Holder
Recipes: Murdoch Books Test Kitchen
Food editor: Kathy Knudsen
Photographer: Prue Ruscoe
Extra photography: Ashley Mackevicius
Stylist: Sarah DeNardi
Food preparation: Julie Ray, Ross Dobson
Production: Monika Vidovic